TEACHER GUIDE FOR

THIS PLACE

150 Years Retold

TEACHER GUIDE FOR

THIS PLACE

150 Years Retold

Created by Christine M'Lot

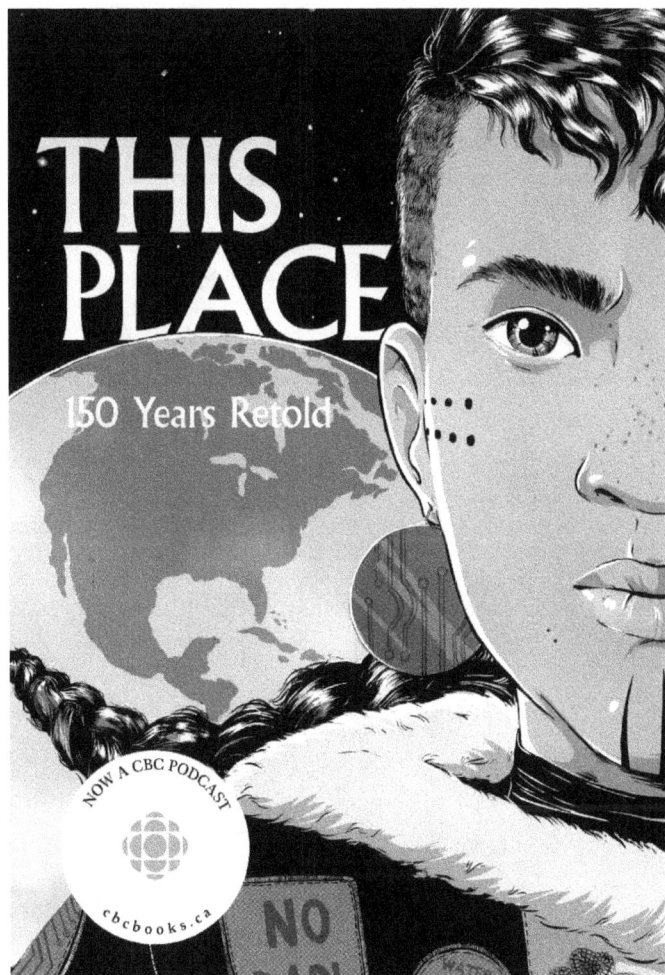

PORTAGE &
MAIN PRESS

© 2021 Christine M'Lot (text)

Portage & Main Press gratefully acknowledges the financial support of the Government of Canada as well as the Province of Manitoba through the Department of Sport, Culture, Heritage and Tourism and the Manitoba Book Publishing Tax Credit for our publishing activities.

Funded by the Government of Canada
Financé par le gouvernement du Canada | Canada

First published as *This Place: 150 Years Retold Teacher Guide* in 2020.
This revised edition includes a new lesson (12)
as well as revisions to the Introduction and curriculum charts.

Design by Jennifer Lum
Cover Art by Natasha Donovan

Thank you to all the authors and illustrators who worked tirelessly,
researching and retelling these incredible stories to ensure they
continue to be passed down through generations.
—CM

ISBN: 978-1-77492-017-6
Also issued in electronic format: ISBN 978-1-77492-018-3 (PDF)

27 26 25 24   2 3 4 5 6

PORTAGE &
MAIN PRESS
www.portageandmainpress.com
Winnipeg, Manitoba
Treaty 1 Territory and homeland of the Métis Nation

CONTENTS

USING THIS GUIDE

T HIS TEACHER'S GUIDE is meant to be a no-prep resource for educators to use either for individual, stand-alone lessons or as a complete unit plan. Throughout the lessons, students will be learning about, exploring, researching, and presenting on essential themes that arise in this graphic novel anthology.

This teacher's guide is best suited for use in courses such as Grades 9–12 English, Grade 11 History, Grade 12 Global Issues and Grade 12 Current Topics in First Nations, Métis, and Inuit Studies. The lesson plans are formatted using the Activate, Acquire, Apply, and Assess (AAAA) format for ease of use. Activate activities are used to assess prior knowledge on a topic or to introduce themes in the lesson. Acquire activities will include learning about various topics related to the graphic novel. Apply activities give the students the opportunity to demonstrate learning, while Assess activities have students complete an assignment to demonstrate the appropriate learning outcomes. All rubrics are included in this guide.

Many activities throughout the lessons infuse Indigenous pedagogical practice by having students work collaboratively. Other activities have students take on the role of expert and teacher, which often involves student-led research. Working in relation with others, seeking holism in understanding, and learning through storytelling are key practices in Indigenous pedagogy. This teacher's guide aims to serve as a tool for engaging students in the complexity of understanding and embracing worldviews that may be different from their own. Other helpful resources related to Indigenous pedagogy include:

- *Potlatch as Pedagogy: Learning Through Ceremony* by Sara Florence Davidson and Robert Davidson
- *Ensouling Our Schools: A Universally Designed Framework for Mental Health, Well-Being, and Reconciliation* by Jennifer Katz with Kevin Lamoureux
- *Truth and Reconciliation in Canadian Schools* by Pamela Rose Toulouse
- *Achieving Indigenous Student Success: A Guide for Secondary Classrooms* by Pamela Rose Toulouse
- Manitoba First Nation Education Resource Centre <https://mfnerc.org/>
- Indspire <https://indspire.ca/for-educators/>
- National Centre for Truth and Reconciliation <https://education.nctr.ca/link-to-page-2/>

TEACHER GUIDE FOR THIS PLACE: 150 YEARS RETOLD © 2021 PORTAGE & MAIN PRESS ISBN: 978-1-77492-017-6

CONSIDERATIONS FOR TEACHING GRAPHIC NOVELS AND PODCASTS

The terms *graphic novel* and *comic* describe the format of a book, rather than a genre. Graphic novels and comic books can be fiction, non-fiction, biography, fantasy, dystopia, or any genre in between.[1] Graphic novels are an accessible reading resource for all students, and they have been proven to engage even the most reluctant of readers.[2] Graphic novels also include dialogue, characters' thoughts, narration, and captions. Graphic novels are meant to be read from left to right, and top to bottom.

The first lesson in this guide is designed to introduce teachers and students alike to this format, and the final lesson is designed to introduce the format of the podcast. For more information and ideas for using graphic novels in the classroom, see the resource *Teaching With Graphic Novels* by Shelley Stagg Peterson, available through Portage & Main Press.

INDIGENOUS PERSPECTIVES AND HISTORY

Indigenous perspectives are now part of the curriculum in every province in Canada. Further, the National Truth and Reconciliation Commission's Calls to Action #62 and #63 deal directly with Indigenous education, stating:

62. We call upon the federal, provincial, and territorial governments, in consultation and collaboration with Survivors, Aboriginal peoples, and educators, to:

   i   Make age-appropriate curriculum on residential schools, Treaties, and Aboriginal peoples' historical and contemporary contributions to Canada a mandatory education requirement for Kindergarten to Grade Twelve students.

   ii   Provide the necessary funding to post-secondary institutions to educate teachers on how to integrate Indigenous knowledge and teaching methods into classrooms.

   iii   Provide the necessary funding to Aboriginal schools to utilize Indigenous knowledge and teaching methods in classrooms.

   iv   Establish senior-level positions in government at the assistant deputy minister level or higher dedicated to Aboriginal content in education.

TEACHER GUIDE FOR THIS PLACE: 150 YEARS RETOLD © 2021 PORTAGE & MAIN PRESS   ISBN: 978-1-77492-017-6

1   "What is a Graphic Novel?" Get Graphic, the Buffalo and Erie County Public Library and Partnering Organizations, accessed April 20, 2020, https://www.buffalolib.org/get-graphic/what-graphic-novel

2   Knutson, Sarah. "How Graphic Novels Help Students Develop Critical Skills," Room 241: A Blog by Concordia University-Portland, updated October 23, 2018, https://education.cu-portland.edu/blog/classroom-resources/graphic-novels-visual-literacy/.

63. We call upon the Council of Ministers of Education, Canada to maintain an annual commitment to Aboriginal education issues, including:

   i Developing and implementing Kindergarten to Grade Twelve curriculum and learning resources on Aboriginal peoples in Canadian history, and the history and legacy of residential schools.

   ii Sharing information and best practices on teaching curriculum related to residential schools and Aboriginal history.

   iii Building student capacity for intercultural understanding, empathy, and mutual respect.

   iv Identifying teacher-training needs relating to the above.[3]

For too long, Indigenous stories have been misinterpreted and misrepresented, and in recent years, there has been a resurgence of Indigenous people reclaiming their own stories, hence the word *retold* in the title of this graphic novel. *This Place: 150 Years Retold* is recommended for use with students in grades 9–12, as it includes a variety of historical and contemporary stories that highlight important moments in Indigenous history. Moreover, this resource proves valuable in introducing students to the demographic, historical, and cultural uniqueness among Indigenous groups, and it is an exceptional resource for exposing students to specific acts of sovereignty and resiliency in Indigenous and Canadian history.

Aspects of Indigenous pedagogy are woven throughout this teacher's guide to enhance students' understanding of Indigenous worldviews. Circle pedagogy is used throughout this resource as a way to show the interconnectedness of ideas and topics, namely in the form of the medicine wheel as a graphic organizer. The medicine wheel is an ancient symbol representing interconnectedness, balance, and holism that has been adapted for modern audiences as a graphic organizer to visually represent relationships between concepts in groups of four. Finally, students will have the opportunity to select, research, and present on an Indigenous resistance movement that has been successful in challenging the ongoing attempted colonization of Indigenous peoples.

According to the Manitoba Education and Youth's *Integrating Aboriginal Perspectives into Curricula* document (2003), implementing Indigenous perspectives has a number of positive effects in the classroom including:

- helping Indigenous students develop a positive self-identity through learning their own histories, cultures, traditional values, contemporary lifestyles, and traditional knowledge
- helping Indigenous students to participate in a learning environment that will equip them with the knowledge and skills needed to participate more fully in the unique civic and cultural realities of their communities

---

3 Truth and Reconciliation Commission of Canada. *Truth and Reconciliation Commission of Canada: Calls to Action.* (2015), 7.

TEACHER GUIDE FOR THIS PLACE: 150 YEARS RETOLD © 2021 PORTAGE & MAIN PRESS ISBN: 978-1-77492-017-6

- helping non-Indigenous students develop an understanding and respect for the histories, traditional values, contemporary lifestyles, and traditional knowledge of Indigenous peoples
- helping non-Indigenous students develop informed opinions on matters relating to Indigenous peoples[4]

CONSIDERATIONS FOR TEACHING *THIS PLACE: 150 YEARS RETOLD*

Sensitive themes are likely to come up when reading *This Place: 150 Years Retold* and learning about Indigenous topics. This graphic novel anthology deals with sensitive topics such as racism, suicide, violence and abuse, the child welfare system, and even cannibalism. It is important that you inform your students about resources that are available to them if they should feel overwhelmed or triggered at any point throughout the readings. Teachers should also create a safe and open learning environment where students' mental health is supported. Often, having direct discussions about mental health and wellness is a great way for students to hear from others and learn positive coping skills to help them through their learning journeys. Lesson 7: How Can We Practise Wellness? (Nimkii) touches on the subject of wellness through an Indigenous lens and guides students through a medicine-wheel wellness activity.

INVITING AN ELDER INTO YOUR LEARNING SPACE

Teachers may want to engage the larger community and invite an Elder or Knowledge Keeper into their classroom to share stories, knowledge, or teachings with the class. Manitoba Education and Youth defines an Elder as "any person regarded or chosen by an Aboriginal Nation to be the keeper and teacher of its oral tradition and knowledge," but it is important to remember that this definition may vary from community to community.[5] The following are some guidelines to help build a positive relationship with a local Elder or Knowledge Keeper.

PREPARING TO MEET WITH AN ELDER
- Ask your local school board if they have an Elder-in-residence or a trusted Elder or Knowledge Keeper that they often ask to speak with students. You should always try to invite a local Elder first.
- Research the local protocols for inviting an Elder to speak with your class. Often, this will involve the passing of tobacco.
- Arrange a meeting between you and the Elder well in advance of the visit to your class.

---

4 Manitoba Education and Youth. *Integrating Aboriginal Perspectives into Curricula: A Resource for Curriculum Developers, Teachers, and Administrators.* 2003.

5 Ibid.

TEACHER GUIDE FOR THIS PLACE: 150 YEARS RETOLD © 2021 PORTAGE & MAIN PRESS ISBN: 978-1-77492-017-6

MEETING WITH AN ELDER

- Share a bit about yourself and your family's history.
- Listen and learn from the Elder.
- Adhere to the protocols in your area, and ask the Elder if they would be interested in sharing their gifts with your class.
- Be as flexible about the day and time for the visit as you can. Decide this together!
- Ask if the Elder needs any special accommodations for when they come.
- Discuss fair compensation. The Elder may be taking the day off from work to accommodate your needs, so it is essential that they are well compensated for their time, energy, and emotional labour.
- Ask the Elder how they would like to be introduced to your class, and respect their preferences.

PREPARING YOUR STUDENTS FOR AN ELDER'S VISIT

- Inform students that an Elder will be visiting the class. Ask if anyone knows what an Elder is, and discuss the important roles they have in Indigenous communities. Share that Elders are people who hold sacred teachings and should be treated with the utmost respect.
- Share with students why you decided to bring an Elder into the classroom.
- Ask if any students would like to volunteer to give the Elder a tobacco tie (depending on the protocol of your region). Brief students about the protocol, and why it is important to thank the Elder in this way.

DAY OF THE VISIT TO YOUR CLASS

- Welcome the Elder to your class/school. Have a student present the Elder with the tobacco tie (depending on the protocol in your region).
- Give the Elder a tour of your school, if possible, or at least make sure they know where the washrooms are.
- Ensure that students are respectful while the Elder is speaking.
- Thank the Elder at the end and present them with the honorarium.

Try to build a relationship with a local Elder or Knowledge Keeper. Relationships take time to develop, so you should contact the Elder as soon as possible. If the day goes well, make sure to let them know that you will be inviting them back again. You could also have students write a thank-you card to the Elder as a way of showing appreciation.

TEACHER GUIDE FOR THIS PLACE: 150 YEARS RETOLD © 2021 PORTAGE & MAIN PRESS ISBN: 978-1-77492-017-6

CURRICULUM CONNECTIONS

BRITISH COLUMBIA: ENGLISH FIRST PEOPLES LITERARY STUDIES 10

	Lesson											
	1	2	3	4	5	6	7	8	9	10	11	12
Curricular Competencies[6] Using oral, written, visual, and digital texts, students are expected individually and collaboratively to be able to:												
Recognize and appreciate the role of story, narrative, and oral tradition in expressing First Peoples perspectives, values, beliefs, and points of view	X	X	X	X	X	X	X	X	X	X	X	X
Recognize and appreciate the diversity within and across First Peoples societies as represented in texts	X	X	X	X	X	X	X	X	X	X	X	X
Apply appropriate strategies in a variety of contexts to guide inquiry, extend thinking, and comprehend texts			X	X	X				X	X	X	X
Construct meaningful personal connections between self, text, and world	X	X	X	X	X	X	X	X	X	X	X	X
Think critically, creatively, and reflectively to explore ideas within, between, and beyond texts	X	X	X	X	X			X	X	X	X	X

6   Based on *BC's New Curriculum: English First Peoples Literary Studies 10*. Accessed March 24, 2020. https://curriculum.gov.bc.ca/curriculum/english-language-arts/10/efp-literary-studies

	Lesson											
	1	2	3	4	5	6	7	8	9	10	11	12
Recognize and appreciate how different forms, structures, and features of texts reflect diverse purposes, audiences, and messages	X	X	X	X	X	X	X	X	X	X	X	X
Recognize the impact of personal, social, and cultural identities in First Peoples texts		X	X	X	X	X	X	X	X	X	X	X
Examine how literary elements, techniques, and devices enhance and shape meaning and impact	X	X	X	X	X	X	X	X	X	X	X	X
Assess the authenticity of First Peoples texts		X	X	X	X	X	X	X	X	X	X	X
Respectfully exchange ideas and viewpoints from diverse perspectives to build shared understandings and extend thinking		X		X	X			X		X	X	
Respond to text in personal, creative, and critical ways	X	X	X	X	X	X	X	X	X	X	X	X
Demonstrate speaking and listening skills in a variety of formal and informal contexts for a range of purposes		X	X	X			X			X	X	X
Use the conventions of First Peoples and other Canadian spelling, syntax, and diction proficiently and as appropriate to the context	X	X	X	X	X	X	X	X	X	X	X	X
Express an opinion and support it with evidence		X		X				X	X	X		X

TEACHER GUIDE FOR THIS PLACE: 150 YEARS RETOLD © 2021 PORTAGE & MAIN PRESS ISBN: 978-1-77492-017-6

TEACHER GUIDE FOR THIS PLACE: 150 YEARS RETOLD © 2021 PORTAGE & MAIN PRESS   ISBN: 978-1-77492-017-6

	Lesson											
	1	2	3	4	5	6	7	8	9	10	11	12
Use writing and design processes to plan, develop, and create engaging and meaningful texts for a variety of purposes and audiences		X		X	X				X	X	X	X
Assess and refine texts to improve clarity and impact		X		X	X				X	X	X	X

Content
Students are expected to know the following:

	1	2	3	4	5	6	7	8	9	10	11	12
Text forms and genres	X	X	X	X	X	X	X	X	X	X	X	X
Common themes in First Peoples texts	X	X	X	X	X	X	X	X	X	X	X	X
First Peoples oral traditions • purposes of First Peoples oral text		X				X			X			X
Text features and structures • narrative structures, including those found in First Peoples texts • form, function, and genre of texts	X	X	X	X	X	X	X	X	X	X	X	X
Strategies and processes • reading strategies • metacognitive strategies • writing processes • oral language strategies	X	X	X	X	X	X	X	X	X	X	X	X
Language features, structures, and conventions • elements of style • usage and conventions • literary elements and devices • citations and acknowledgements • literal and inferential meaning	X	X	X	X	X	X	X	X	X	X	X	X

BRITISH COLUMBIA: ENGLISH FIRST PEOPLES LITERARY STUDIES + SPOKEN LANGUAGE 11

	Lesson											
	1	2	3	4	5	6	7	8	9	10	11	12
Curricular Competencies[7] Using oral, written, visual, and digital texts, students are expected individually and collaboratively to be able to:												
Demonstrate understanding of how First Peoples languages and texts reflect their cultures, knowledge, histories, and worldviews		X	X	X	X	X	X	X	X	X	X	X
Access information for diverse purposes and from a variety of sources to inform development of oral texts		X		X				X				
Apply appropriate strategies in a variety of contexts to guide inquiry, extend thinking, and comprehend oral and other texts	X	X	X	X	X	X	X	X	X	X	X	X
Recognize and appreciate how different forms, formats, structures, and features of texts reflect different purposes, audiences, and messages	X	X	X	X	X	X	X	X	X	X	X	X
Think critically, creatively, and reflectively to explore ideas within, between, and beyond texts	X	X	X	X	X	X	X	X	X	X	X	X
Recognize and identify personal, social, and cultural contexts, values, and perspectives in oral and other texts, including gender, sexual orientation, and socioeconomic factors		X	X	X	X	X	X	X	X	X	X	X

TEACHER GUIDE FOR THIS PLACE: 150 YEARS RETOLD © 2021 PORTAGE & MAIN PRESS   ISBN: 978-1-77492-017-6

7 Based on *BC's New Curriculum: English First Peoples Literary Studies + Spoken Language 11*. Accessed March 24, 2020. https://curriculum.gov.
bc.ca/curriculum/english-language-arts/11/efp-literary-studies-and-spoken-language

TEACHER GUIDE FOR THIS PLACE: 150 YEARS RETOLD © 2021 PORTAGE & MAIN PRESS   ISBN: 978-1-77492-017-6

	Lesson											
	1	2	3	4	5	6	7	8	9	10	11	12
Demonstrate understanding of how language constructs and reflects personal, social, and cultural identities	X	X	X	X	X	X	X	X	X	X	X	X
Construct meaningful personal connections between self, text, and world	X	X	X	X	X	X	X	X	X	X	X	X
Recognize and understand the roles of story and oral traditions in expressing First Peoples perspectives, values, beliefs, and points of view		X	X	X	X	X	X	X	X	X	X	X
Understand and evaluate how literary elements, techniques, and devices enhance and shape meaning and impact	X	X	X	X	X	X	X	X	X	X	X	X
Recognize and understand the diversity within and across First Peoples societies as represented in texts		X	X	X	X	X	X	X	X	X	X	X
Assess the authenticity of First Peoples texts		X	X	X	X	X	X	X	X	X	X	X
Understand the influence of land/place in First Peoples oral and other texts		X	X	X	X	X	X	X	X	X	X	
Respectfully exchange ideas and viewpoints from diverse perspectives to build shared understandings and extend thinking		X	X		X	X		X	X	X	X	
Demonstrate speaking and listening skills in a variety of formal and informal contexts for a range of purposes		X	X	X	X	X	X	X	X	X	X	

	Lesson											
	1	2	3	4	5	6	7	8	9	10	11	12
Select and apply appropriate spoken language formats for intended purposes	X	X	X	X		X		X		X		
Express and support an opinion with evidence	X	X	X	X	X	X	X	X	X	X	X	X
Respond to text in personal, creative, and critical ways	X	X	X	X	X	X	X	X	X	X	X	X
Use writing and design processes to plan, develop, and create engaging and meaningful texts for a variety of purposes and audiences	X		X		X	X			X	X	X	X
Use creative processes to plan, develop, and create engaging and meaningful oral texts for a variety of purposes and audiences			X	X	X				X	X	X	
Assess and refine oral and other texts to improve clarity, effectiveness, and impact			X	X	X				X	X	X	
Use a variety of techniques to engage listeners			X	X	X				X	X	X	
Experiment with genres, forms, or styles of oral and other texts	X	X	X	X	X	X	X	X	X	X	X	X
Use the conventions of First Peoples and other Canadian spelling, syntax, and diction proficiently and as appropriate to the context	X	X	X	X	X	X	X	X	X	X	X	X
Recognize intellectual property rights and community protocols and apply them as necessary		X	X	X	X	X	X	X	X	X	X	X

TEACHER GUIDE FOR THIS PLACE: 150 YEARS RETOLD © 2021 PORTAGE & MAIN PRESS ISBN: 978-1-77492-017-6

	Lesson											
	1	2	3	4	5	6	7	8	9	10	11	12
Content Students are expected to know the following:												
A wide variety of BC, Canadian, and global First Peoples texts	X	X	X	X	X	X	X	X	X	X	X	X
A wide variety of text forms and genre	X	X	X	X	X	X	X	X	X	X	X	X
Common themes in First Peoples texts		X	X	X	X	X	X	X	X	X	X	X
First Peoples oral traditions • the legal status of First Peoples oral traditions in Canada • purposes of oral texts • the relationship between oral tradition and land/place		X	X	X	X	X	X	X	X	X		
Protocols • protocols related to the ownership and use of First Peoples oral texts • acknowledgement of territory • situating oneself in relation to others and place • processes related to protocols and expectations when engaging with First Nations communities and Aboriginal organizations		X	X	X	X	X	X	X	X	X		
Text features and structures • narrative structures, including those found in First Peoples texts • form, function, and genre of oral and other texts	X	X	X	X	X	X	X	X	X	X	X	X

	Lesson											
	1	2	3	4	5	6	7	8	9	10	11	12
Strategies and processes • reading strategies • oral language strategies • metacognitive strategies • writing processes • oral storytelling techniques • presentation and performance strategies	X	X	X	X	X	X	X	X	X	X	X	X
Language features, structures, and conventions • features of oral language • elements of style • syntax and fluency • rhetorical devices • usage and conventions • literary elements and devices • literal and inferential meaning • persuasive techniques • citations and acknowledgements	X	X	X	X	X	X	X	X	X	X	X	X

TEACHER GUIDE FOR THIS PLACE: 150 YEARS RETOLD © 2021 PORTAGE & MAIN PRESS ISBN: 978-1-77492-017-6

BRITISH COLUMBIA: ENGLISH FIRST PEOPLES 12

TEACHER GUIDE FOR THIS PLACE: 150 YEARS RETOLD © 2021 PORTAGE & MAIN PRESS ISBN: 978-1-77492-017-6

	Lesson											
	1	2	3	4	5	6	7	8	9	10	11	12
Curricular Competencies[8] Using oral, written, visual, and digital texts, students are expected individually and collaboratively to be able to:												
Analyze how First Peoples languages and texts reflect their cultures, knowledge, histories, and worldviews		X	X	X	X	X	X	X	X	X	X	X
Access information for diverse purposes and from a variety of sources and evaluate its relevance accuracy, and reliability		X		X				X				X
Select and apply appropriate strategies in a variety of contexts to guide inquiry, extend thinking, and comprehend texts	X	X	X	X	X	X	X	X	X	X	X	X
Analyze how different forms, formats, structures, and features of texts reflect different purposes, audiences, and messages	X	X	X	X	X	X	X	X	X	X	X	X
Think critically, creatively, and reflectively to explore ideas within, between, and beyond texts	X	X	X	X	X	X	X	X	X	X	X	X
Recognize and identify personal, social, and cultural contexts, values, and perspectives in texts, including gender, sexual orientation, and socioeconomic factors		X	X	X	X	X	X	X	X	X	X	X

8 Based on *BC's New Curriculum: English First Peoples 12*. Accessed March 24, 2020. https://curriculum.gov.bc.ca/curriculum/english-language-arts/12/english-first-peoples

	Lesson											
	1	2	3	4	5	6	7	8	9	10	11	12
Appreciate and understand how language constructs and reflects personal, social, and cultural identities	X	X	X	X	X	X	X	X	X	X	X	X
Construct meaningful personal connections between self, text, and world	X	X	X	X	X	X	X	X	X	X	X	X
Demonstrate understanding of the role of story and oral traditions in expressing First Peoples perspectives, values, beliefs, and points of view		X	X	X	X	X	X	X	X	X	X	X
Understand and evaluate how literary elements, techniques, and devices enhance and shape meaning and impact	X	X	X	X	X	X	X	X	X	X	X	X
Recognize and understand the diversity within and across First Peoples societies as represented in texts		X	X	X	X	X	X	X	X	X	X	X
Analyze the diversity within and across First Peoples societies as represented in texts					X			X	X	X		X
Assess the authenticity of First Peoples texts		X	X	X	X	X	X	X	X	X	X	
Analyze the influence of land/place in First Peoples texts		X	X	X	X	X	X	X	X	X	X	
Examine the significance of terms/words from First Peoples languages used in English texts		X	X	X	X	X	X	X	X	X	X	

TEACHER GUIDE FOR THIS PLACE: 150 YEARS RETOLD © 2021 PORTAGE & MAIN PRESS ISBN-978-1-77492-017-6

	Lesson											
	1	2	3	4	5	6	7	8	9	10	11	12
Discern nuances in the meanings of words, considering social, political, historical, and literary contexts		X	X	X	X	X	X	X	X	X	X	X
Respectfully exchange ideas and viewpoints from diverse perspectives to build shared understandings and extend thinking		X	X		X	X		X	X	X	X	
Demonstrate speaking and listening skills in a variety of formal and informal contexts for a range of purposes		X	X	X	X	X	X	X	X	X	X	X
Select and apply appropriate oral communication formats for intended purposes	X	X	X	X		X		X		X		
Express and support an opinion with evidence	X	X	X	X	X	X	X	X	X	X	X	X
Respond to text in personal, creative, and critical ways	X	X	X	X	X	X	X	X	X	X	X	X
Use writing and design processes to plan, develop, and create engaging and meaningful texts for a variety of purposes and audiences	X		X		X	X			X	X	X	X
Assess and refine texts to improve clarity, effectiveness, and impact			X	X	X				X	X	X	X
Experiment with genres, forms, or styles of texts	X	X	X	X	X	X	X	X	X	X	X	X
Use the conventions of First Peoples and other Canadian spelling, syntax, and diction proficiently and as appropriate to the context	X	X	X	X	X	X	X	X	X	X	X	X

	Lesson											
	1	2	3	4	5	6	7	8	9	10	11	12
Transform ideas and information to create original texts, using various genres, forms, structures, and styles	X	X	X	X	X	X	X	X	X	X	X	X
Recognize intellectual property rights and community protocols and apply as necessary		X	X	X	X	X	X	X	X	X	X	

Content
Students are expected to know the following:

	1	2	3	4	5	6	7	8	9	10	11	12
A wide variety of BC, Canadian, and global First Peoples texts	X	X	X	X	X	X	X	X	X	X	X	X
A wide variety of text forms and genres	X	X	X	X	X	X	X	X	X	X	X	X
Common themes in First Peoples literature		X	X	X	X	X	X	X	X	X	X	X
First Peoples oral traditions • the legal status of First Peoples oral traditions in Canada • purposes of oral texts • the relationship between oral tradition and land/place		X	X	X	X	X	X	X	X	X		
Protocols • protocols related to the ownership and use of First Peoples oral texts • acknowledgement of territory • situating oneself in relation to others and place • processes related to protocols and expectations when engaging with First Nations communities and Aboriginal organizations		X	X	X	X	X	X	X	X	X		

TEACHER GUIDE FOR THIS PLACE: 150 YEARS RETOLD © 2021 PORTAGE & MAIN PRESS ISBN: 978-1-77492-017-6

	Lesson											
	1	**2**	**3**	**4**	**5**	**6**	**7**	**8**	**9**	**10**	**11**	**12**
Text features and structures • narrative structures, including those found in First Peoples texts • form, function, and genre of texts	X	X	X	X	X	X	X	X	X	X	X	X
Strategies and processes • reading strategies • oral language strategies • metacognitive strategies • writing processes • presentation techniques	X	X	X	X	X	X	X	X	X	X	X	X
Language features, structures, and conventions • features of oral language • elements of style • language change • syntax and sentence fluency • rhetorical devices • usage and conventions • literary elements and devices • literal and inferential meaning • persuasive techniques • citations and acknowledgements	X	X	X	X	X	X	X	X	X	X	X	X

TEACHER GUIDE FOR THIS PLACE: 150 YEARS RETOLD © 2021 PORTAGE & MAIN PRESS ISBN: 978-1-77492-017-6

MANITOBA: SENIOR 1 ENGLISH LANGUAGE ARTS

	Lesson											
	1	2	3	4	5	6	7	8	9	10	11	12
Curriculum Outcomes[9]												
1.1.1 Express Ideas Question and reflect on personal responses, predictions, and interpretations; apply personal viewpoints to diverse situations or circumstances.		X	X	X	X	X	X	X	X	X	X	X
1.1.2 Consider Others' Ideas Acknowledge the value of others' ideas and opinions in exploring and extending personal interpretations and viewpoints.		X	X	X		X	X			X	X	X
1.1.3 Experiment with Language and Form Use memorable language effectively and experiment with different personas for dynamic self-expression.		X	X	X	X	X			X	X	X	
1.2.1 Develop Understanding Reflect on new understanding in relation to prior knowledge and identify gaps in personal knowledge.	X	X	X	X	X	X	X	X	X	X	X	X
1.2.2 Explain Opinions Review and refine personal viewpoints through reflection, feedback, and self-assessment.		X		X	X		X	X	X	X	X	X

---

9 Based on the 1996 edition of *Senior 1 English Language Arts: Manitoba Curriculum Framework of Outcomes and Senior 1 Standards.* https://www.edu.gov.mb.ca/k12/cur/ela/docs/s1_framework/index.html

TEACHER GUIDE FOR THIS PLACE: 150 YEARS RETOLD © 2021 PORTAGE & MAIN PRESS ISBN: 978-1-77492-017-6

	Lesson											
	1	2	3	4	5	6	7	8	9	10	11	12
1.2.4 Extend Understanding Consider diverse opinions, explore ambiguities, and assess whether new information clarifies understanding.		X	X	X	X	X	X	X	X	X	X	X
2.1.1 Prior Knowledge Analyze and explain connections between previous experiences, prior knowledge, and a variety of texts [including books].		X	X	X	X	X	X	X	X	X	X	X
2.1.2 Comprehension Strategies Use comprehension strategies [including recognizing main ideas and significant supporting details, and paraphrasing ideas] appropriate to the type of text and purpose; enhance understanding by rereading and discussing relevant passages.		X	X	X	X	X		X	X	X	X	X
2.1.3 Textual Cues Use textual cues and prominent organizational patterns within texts to construct and confirm meaning and interpret texts.			X		X	X		X	X	X	X	X
2.2.2 Connect Self, Texts and Culture Examine how personal experiences, community traditions, and Canadian perspectives are presented in oral, literary, and media texts.		X	X	X	X	X	X	X	X	X	X	X

TEACHER GUIDE FOR THIS PLACE: 150 YEARS RETOLD © 2021 PORTAGE & MAIN PRESS ISBN: 978-1-77492-017-6

	Lesson											
	1	2	3	4	5	6	7	8	9	10	11	12
2.3.5 Create Original Texts Create original texts to communicate and demonstrate understanding of forms and techniques.			X		X	X			X	X	X	X
3.1.3 Participate in Group Inquiry Generate and access ideas in a group and use a variety of methods to focus and clarify inquiry or research topic.		X		X			X	X		X		
3.3.1 Organize Information Organize information and ideas by developing and selecting appropriate categories and organizational structures.			X	X	X	X	X	X	X	X	X	X
3.3.2 Record Information Summarize and record information in a variety of forms in own words, paraphrasing and/or quoting relevant facts and opinions; reference sources.			X	X	X	X	X	X	X	X	X	X
4.2.2. Revise Content Analyze and revise drafts to ensure appropriate content, accuracy, clarity, and completeness.			X	X	X	X			X	X	X	X
4.2.3 Enhance Legibility Use appropriate text features to enhance legibility for particular audiences, purposes, and contexts.			X		X	X			X	X	X	
4.3.1 Grammar and Usage Edit for parallel structure, use of transitional devices, and clarity.			X		X	X			X	X	X	X

TEACHER GUIDE FOR THIS PLACE: 150 YEARS RETOLD © 2021 PORTAGE & MAIN PRESS ISBN: 978-1-77492-017-6

TEACHER GUIDE FOR THIS PLACE: 150 YEARS RETOLD © 2021 PORTAGE & MAIN PRESS ISBN: 978-1-77492-017-6

	Lesson											
	1	2	3	4	5	6	7	8	9	10	11	12
4.3.2 Spelling Know and apply a repertoire of spelling conventions when editing and proofreading; use a variety of resources when editing and proofreading.			X		X	X			X	X	X	X
4.3.3 Capitalization and Punctuation Know and apply capitalization and punctuation conventions in dialogues, quotations, footnotes, endnotes, and references when editing and proofreading.			X		X	X			X	X	X	X
4.4.2 Effective Oral Communication Choose vocabulary, voice production factors, and nonverbal cues to communicate effectively to a variety of audiences; use a variety of media and display techniques to enhance the effectiveness of oral presentations.		X		X	X			X	X	X	X	
5.1.1 Cooperate with Others Recognize the importance of effective communication in working with others.		X		X	X			X	X	X	X	
5.1.2 Work in Groups Plan, organize, and participate in presentations of group finding.		X		X				X			X	
5.2.1. Compare Responses Recognize that differing perspectives and unique reactions enrich understanding.		X		X				X	X		X	

MANITOBA: GRADE 9 SOCIAL STUDIES

	Lesson											
	1	2	3	4	5	6	7	8	9	10	11	12
Curriculum Outcomes[10]												
S-100 Collaborate with others to achieve group goals and responsibilities.		X		X			X			X	X	
S-200 Select information from a variety of oral, visual, material, print, or electronic sources, including primary and secondary.	X	X	X	X	X	X	X	X	X	X	X	X
S-201 Organize and record information in a variety of formats and reference sources appropriately.	X	X	X	X	X	X	X	X	X	X	X	X
S-204 Select, use, and interpret various types of maps.		X	X	X	X	X	X	X	X	X	X	
S-300 Plan topics, goals, and methods for inquiry and research.		X	X	X	X	X	X	X	X	X	X	X
S-301 Analyze the context of events, accounts, ideas, and interpretations.		X	X	X	X	X	X	X	X	X	X	X
S-303 Reconsider personal assumptions based on new information and ideas.		X	X	X	X	X	X	X	X	X	X	X
S-305 Compare diverse perspectives and interpretations in the media and other information sources.	X	X	X	X	X	X	X	X	X	X	X	X
S-400 Listen to others to understand their perspectives.		X		X						X	X	

---

10 Based on the 2007 edition of *Grade 9 Social Studies Canada in the Contemporary World: A Foundation for Implementation*.
https://www.edu.gov.mb.ca/k12/cur/socstud/foundation_gr9/index.html

TEACHER GUIDE FOR THIS PLACE: 150 YEARS RETOLD © 2021 PORTAGE & MAIN PRESS ISBN: 978-1-77492-017-6

TEACHER GUIDE FOR THIS PLACE: 150 YEARS RETOLD © 2021 PORTAGE & MAIN PRESS ISBN: 978-1-77492-017-6

	Lesson											
	1	2	3	4	5	6	7	8	9	10	11	12
S-402 Express informed and reasoned opinions.		X		X						X	X	X
S-403 Present information and ideas in a variety of formats appropriate for audience and purpose.	X	X	X	X	X	X	X	X	X	X	X	X
S-404 Elicit, clarify, and respond to questions, ideas, and diverse points of view in discussions.	X	X	X	X	X	X	X	X	X	X	X	X
S-405 Articulate their perspectives on issues.		X		X						X	X	X
S-406 Debate differing points of view regarding an issue.				X								
KC-009 Identify contemporary political leaders in Canada.		X										
KC-010A Describe Aboriginal perspectives on justice and law.										X		
KI-017 Give examples of ways in which First Nations, Inuit, and Métis peoples are rediscovering their cultures.						X	X					
KI-018 Evaluate effects of assimilative policies on cultural and linguistic groups in Canada.			X	X	X	X	X	X	X			
VI-005A Be willing to support the vitality of their First Nations, Inuit, or Métis languages and cultures.		X	X	X	X	X	X	X	X	X	X	

	Lesson											
	1	2	3	4	5	6	7	8	9	10	11	12
KL-027 Give examples of opportunities and challenges related to First Nations treaties and Aboriginal rights.			X	X	X	X	X	X	X			
VL-006 Respect traditional relationships that Aboriginal peoples of Canada have with the land.		X	X	X	X	X	X	X	X			
KH-030 Describe social and cultural injustices in Canada's past.		X	X	X	X	X	X	X	X	X		X
KP-043 Give examples of diverse approaches to conflict resolution.		X	X		X		X	X	X	X		
KP-045 Describe factors related to Aboriginal self-determination in Canada.		X	X	X	X	X	X	X	X	X		
VP-014 Value non-violent resolutions to conflict.		X	X		X		X	X	X	X		

TEACHER GUIDE FOR THIS PLACE: 150 YEARS RETOLD © 2021 PORTAGE & MAIN PRESS ISBN: 978-1-77492-017-6

MANITOBA: SENIOR 2 ENGLISH LANGUAGE ARTS

Curriculum Outcomes[11]	Lesson											
	1	2	3	4	5	6	7	8	9	10	11	12
1.1.1 Express Ideas Consider the potential of emerging ideas through a variety of means to develop tentative positions.		X	X	X	X	X	X	X	X	X	X	X
1.1.2 Consider Others' Ideas Seek and consider others' ideas through a variety of means to expand understanding.		X	X	X		X	X			X	X	X
1.1.3 Experiment with Language and Form Demonstrate a willingness to take risks in language use and experiment with language and forms of expression.		X	X	X	X	X			X	X	X	
1.2.2 Explain Opinions Explain opinions, providing support or reasons; anticipate other viewpoints.		X			X	X		X	X	X	X	X
1.2.4 Extend Understanding Explore ways in which real and vicarious experiences and various perspectives affect understanding when generating and responding to texts.		X	X	X	X	X	X	X	X	X	X	X

---

11 Based on the 1998 edition of *Senior 2 English Language Arts: Manitoba Curriculum Framework of Outcomes*.
https://www.edu.gov.mb.ca/k12/ cur/ela/docs/s2_framework/index.html

TEACHER GUIDE FOR THIS PLACE: 150 YEARS RETOLD © 2021 PORTAGE & MAIN PRESS ISBN: 978-1-77492-017-6

	Lesson											
	1	2	3	4	5	6	7	8	9	10	11	12
2.1.1 Prior Knowledge Apply personal experiences and prior knowledge of language and texts to develop understanding and interpretations of a variety of texts [including books].		X	X	X	X	X	X	X	X	X	X	X
2.1.2 Comprehension Strategies Select, describe, and use comprehension strategies to monitor understanding and develop interpretations of a variety of texts.		X	X	X	X	X		X	X	X	X	X
2.1.3 Textual Cues Use textual cues and prominent organizational patterns to construct and confirm meaning and interpret texts.			X		X	X		X	X	X	X	X
2.2.2 Connect Self, Texts and Culture Respond personally and critically to individuals, events, and ideas presented in a variety of Canadian and international texts.		X	X	X	X	X	X	X	X	X	X	X
2.3.5 Create Original Texts Create original texts to communicate ideas and enhance understanding of forms and techniques.			X		X	X			X	X	X	X
3.1.3 Participate in Group Inquiry Collaborate to determine group knowledge base and to define research or inquiry purpose and parameters.		X		X			X	X			X	

TEACHER GUIDE FOR THIS PLACE: 150 YEARS RETOLD © 2021 PORTAGE & MAIN PRESS ISBN: 978-1-77492-017-6

	Lesson											
	1	**2**	**3**	**4**	**5**	**6**	**7**	**8**	**9**	**10**	**11**	**12**
3.3.1 Organize Information Organize information using appropriate forms for specific purposes.			X	X	X	X	X	X	X	X	X	X
3.3.2 Record Information Select and record important information and ideas using an organizational structure appropriate for purpose and information source; document sources accurately.			X	X	X	X	X	X	X	X	X	X
4.2.2. Revise Content Analyze and revise drafts to ensure appropriate content, accuracy, clarity, and completeness.			X	X	X	X			X	X	X	X
4.2.3 Enhance Legibility Use appropriate text features to enhance legibility for particular audiences, purposes, and contexts.			X		X	X			X	X	X	X
4.3.1 Grammar and Usage Select appropriate words, grammatical structures, and register to achieve clarity and desired effect.			X		X	X			X	X	X	X
4.3.2 Spelling Know and apply Canadian spelling conventions for familiar and new vocabulary; monitor for correctness in editing and proofreading using appropriate resources.			X		X	X			X	X	X	X

TEACHER GUIDE FOR THIS PLACE: 150 YEARS RETOLD © 2021 PORTAGE & MAIN PRESS ISBN: 978-1-77492-017-6

	Lesson											
	1	2	3	4	5	6	7	8	9	10	11	12
4.3.3 Capitalization and Punctuation Know and apply capitalization and punctuation conventions to clarify intended meaning, using appropriate resources as required.			X		X	X			X	X	X	X
4.4.2 Effective Oral Communication Use appropriate voice production factors and nonverbal cues to clarify intent in personal and public communication.		X		X	X			X	X	X	X	
5.1.1 Cooperate with Others Make and encourage contributions to assist in developing group ideas; take responsibility for developing and expressing viewpoints.		X		X	X			X	X	X	X	
5.1.2 Work in Groups Demonstrate effective group interaction skills and strategies.		X		X				X			X	
5.2.1. Compare Responses Consider various ideas, evidence, and viewpoints to expand understanding of texts, others, and self.		X		X				X	X		X	

TEACHER GUIDE FOR THIS PLACE: 150 YEARS RETOLD © 2021 PORTAGE & MAIN PRESS ISBN: 978-1-77492-017-6

MANITOBA: SENIOR 2 SOCIAL STUDIES

	Lesson											
	1	2	3	4	5	6	7	8	9	10	11	12
Curriculum Outcomes[12]												
KI-004 Identify Aboriginal perspectives and rights regarding natural resources and their use.			X					X	X	X		
KP-041 Identify ways in which competing interests and needs influence control and use of the land and natural resources in Canada.			X					X	X	X		
VI-003 Be willing to consider diverse views regarding the use of natural resources.			X					X	X	X		
KC-002 Describe sustainability issues related to natural resource extraction and consumption.			X					X	X	X		
KL-024 Give examples of increasing involvement of Aboriginal peoples in business and industry in Canada.			X		X			X	X	X		
KE-048 Use examples to describe advantages and disadvantages of locating a manufacturing industry in a particular area.			X		X			X	X	X		
S-100 Collaborate with others to achieve group goals and responsibilities.		X		X			X			X	X	

TEACHER GUIDE FOR THIS PLACE: 150 YEARS RETOLD © 2021 PORTAGE & MAIN PRESS ISBN: 978-1-77492-017-6

12 Based on the 2006 edition of *Senior 2 Social Studies Geographic Issues of the 21st Century: Manitoba Curriculum Framework of Outcomes and a Foundation for Implementation.* https://www.edu.gov.mb.ca/k12/cur/socstud/frame_found_sr2/index.html

	Lesson											
	1	2	3	4	5	6	7	8	9	10	11	12
S-200 Select information from a variety of oral, visual, material, print, or electronic sources, including primary and secondary.	X	X	X	X	X	X	X	X	X	X	X	X
S-201 Organize and record information in a variety of formats and reference sources appropriately.	X	X	X	X	X	X	X	X	X	X	X	X
S-204 Select, use, and interpret various types of maps.		X	X	X	X	X	X	X	X	X	X	
S-301 Consider the context of events, accounts, ideas, and interpretations.		X	X	X	X	X	X	X	X	X	X	X
S-303 Reconsider personal assumptions based on new information and ideas.		X	X	X	X	X	X	X	X	X	X	X
S-305 Compare diverse perspectives and interpretations in the media and other information sources.		X	X	X	X	X	X	X	X	X	X	X
S-400 Listen to others to understand their perspectives.		X		X						X	X	X
S-402 Express informed and reasoned opinions.		X		X						X	X	X
S-403 Present information and ideas in a variety of formats appropriate for audience and purpose.	X	X	X	X	X	X	X	X	X	X	X	X
S-404 Elicit, clarify, and respond to questions, ideas, and diverse points of view in discussions.	X	X	X	X	X	X	X	X	X	X	X	
S-405 Articulate their perspectives on issues.		X		X						X	X	X
S-406 Debate differing points of view regarding an issue.				X								

TEACHER GUIDE FOR THIS PLACE: 150 YEARS RETOLD © 2021 PORTAGE & MAIN PRESS ISBN-978-1-77492-017-6

MANITOBA: SENIOR 3 ENGLISH LANGUAGE ARTS

	Lesson											
Curriculum Outcomes[13]	1	2	3	4	5	6	7	8	9	10	11	12
1.1.1 Express Ideas Connect ideas, observations, opinions, and emotions through a variety of means to develop a train of thought and test tentative positions.		X	X	X	X	X	X	X	X	X	X	X
1.1.3 Experiment with Language and Form Experiment with language and forms of expression to achieve particular effects.		X	X	X	X	X			X	X	X	
1.2.2 Explain Opinions Explore various viewpoints and consider the consequences of particular positions when generating and responding to texts.		X		X	X		X	X	X	X	X	X
1.2.4 Extend Understanding Extend understanding by exploring and acknowledging multiple perspectives and ambiguities when generating and responding to texts.		X	X	X	X	X	X	X	X	X	X	X

13 Based on the 1999 edition of *Senior 3 English Language Arts: Manitoba Curriculum Framework of Outcomes*. https://www.edu.gov.mb.ca/k12/cur/ela/docs/s3_framework/index.html

	Lesson											
	1	2	3	4	5	6	7	8	9	10	11	12
2.1.1 Prior Knowledge Examine connections between personal experiences and prior knowledge of language and texts to develop understanding and interpretations of a variety of texts [including books].		X	X	X	X	X	X	X	X	X	X	X
2.1.2 Comprehension Strategies Use and adjust comprehension strategies to monitor understanding and develop interpretations of a variety of texts.		X	X	X	X	X		X	X	X	X	X
2.1.3 Textual Cues Use textual cues and prominent organizational patterns to construct and confirm meaning and interpret texts.			X		X	X		X	X	X	X	X
2.2.2 Connect Self, Texts and Culture Respond personally and critically to ideas and values presented in a variety of Canadian and international texts.		X	X	X	X	X	X	X	X	X	X	X
2.3.5 Create Original Texts Create original texts to communicate ideas and enhance understanding of forms and techniques.			X		X	X			X	X	X	X
3.1.3 Participate in Group Inquiry Explore group knowledge and strengths to determine inquiry or research topic, purpose, and procedures.		X		X			X	X			X	

TEACHER GUIDE FOR THIS PLACE: 150 YEARS RETOLD © 2021 PORTAGE & MAIN PRESS ISBN: 978-1-77492-017-6

						Lesson						
	1	2	3	4	5	6	7	8	9	10	11	12
3.3.1 Organize Information Organize and reorganize information and ideas in a variety of ways for different audiences and purposes.			X	X	X	X	X	X	X	X	X	X
3.3.2 Record Information Summarize and record information, ideas, and perspectives from a variety of sources; document sources accurately.			X	X	X	X	X	X	X	X	X	X
4.2.2. Revise Content Analyze and revise drafts to ensure appropriate content and to enhance unity, clarity, and coherence.			X	X	X	X			X	X	X	X
4.2.3 Enhance Legibility Use appropriate text features to enhance legibility for particular audiences, purposes, and contexts.			X		X	X			X	X	X	X
4.3.1 Grammar and Usage Select appropriate words, grammatical structures, and register for audience, purpose, and context.			X		X	X			X	X	X	X
4.3.2 Spelling Know and apply Canadian spelling conventions and monitor for correctness using appropriate resources; recognize adapted spellings for particular effects.			X		X	X			X	X	X	X
4.3.3 Capitalization and Punctuation Know and apply capitalization and punctuation conventions to clarify intended meaning, using appropriate resources as required.			X		X	X			X	X	X	X

	Lesson											
	1	2	3	4	5	6	7	8	9	10	11	12
4.4.2 Effective Oral and Visual Communication Use appropriate voice and visual production factors to communicate and emphasize intent in personal and public communication.		X		X	X			X	X	X	X	
5.1.1 Cooperate with Others Use language to build and maintain collaborative relationships; take responsibility for respectfully questioning others' viewpoints and requesting further explanation.		X		X	X			X	X	X	X	
5.1.2 Work in Groups Demonstrate flexibility in assuming a variety of group roles and take responsibility for tasks that achieve group goals.		X		X				X			X	
5.2.1. Compare Responses Identify various factors that shape understanding of texts, others, and self.		X		X				X	X		X	

TEACHER GUIDE FOR THIS PLACE: 150 YEARS RETOLD © 2021 PORTAGE & MAIN PRESS ISBN: 978-1-77492-017-6

MANITOBA: GRADE 11 HISTORY

	Lesson											
	1	2	3	4	5	6	7	8	9	10	11	12
Curriculum Outcomes[14]												
11.1.1 Who were the First Peoples, and how did they structure their world?			X	X		X	X	X	X	X		
11.1.2 Why did the French and other Europeans come to North America, and how did they interact with First Peoples?		X		X	X	X		X	X	X		
11.2.2 How did the fur trade, European settlement, and the rise of the Métis nation transform life for the peoples of the Northwest?		X										
11.3.1 Why did the Métis resist the westward expansion of Canada, and what were the consequences?		X										
11.3.4 How was Canada's identity as a nation shaped by the First World War?					X							
11.5.3 How are First Nations, Métis, and Inuit peoples seeking a greater degree of cultural, political, and economic self-determination?	X	X	X	X	X	X	X	X	X	X		

14 Based on the 2014 edition of *Grade 11 History of Canada: A Foundation for Implementation.* https://www.edu.gov.mb.ca/k12/cur/socstud/history_gr11/index.html

TEACHER GUIDE FOR THIS PLACE: 150 YEARS RETOLD © 2021 PORTAGE & MAIN PRESS ISBN: 978-1-77492-017-6

MANITOBA: SENIOR 4 ENGLISH LANGUAGE ARTS

	Lesson											
	1	2	3	4	5	6	7	8	9	10	11	12
Curriculum Outcomes[15]												
1.1.1 Express Ideas Connect ideas, observations, opinions, and emotions through a variety of means to develop a train of thought and test tentative positions.	X	X	X	X	X	X	X	X	X	X	X	X
1.1.3 Experiment with Language and Form Experiment with language and forms of expression to achieve particular effects.	X	X	X	X	X				X	X	X	
1.2.2 Explain Opinions Explore various viewpoints and consider the consequences of particular positions when generating and responding to texts.	X			X	X		X	X	X	X	X	X
1.2.4 Extend Understanding Extend understanding by exploring and acknowledging multiple perspectives and ambiguities when generating and responding to texts.	X	X	X	X	X	X	X	X	X	X	X	X
2.1.1 Prior Knowledge Examine connections between personal experiences and prior knowledge of language and texts to develop understanding and interpretations of a variety of texts [including books].	X	X	X	X	X	X	X	X	X	X	X	X

15 Based on the 2000 edition of *Senior 4 English Language Arts: Manitoba Curriculum Framework of Outcomes and Senior 4 Standards.* https://www.edu.gov.mb.ca/k12/cur/ela/docs/s4_framework/index.html

	Lesson											
	1	2	3	4	5	6	7	8	9	10	11	12
2.1.2 Comprehension Strategies Use and adjust comprehension strategies to monitor understanding and develop interpretations of a variety of texts.		X	X	X	X	X		X	X	X	X	X
2.1.3 Textual Cues Use textual cues and prominent organizational patterns to construct and confirm meaning and interpret texts.			X		X	X		X	X	X	X	X
2.2.2 Connect Self, Texts and Culture Respond personally and critically to ideas and values presented in a variety of Canadian and international texts.		X	X	X	X	X	X	X	X	X	X	X
2.3.5 Create Original Texts Create original texts to communicate ideas and enhance understanding of forms and techniques.			X		X	X			X	X	X	X
3.1.3 Participate in Group Inquiry Explore group knowledge and strengths to determine inquiry or research topic, purpose, and procedures.		X		X			X	X			X	
3.3.1 Organize Information Organize and reorganize information and ideas in a variety of ways for different audiences and purposes.			X	X	X	X	X	X	X	X	X	X

TEACHER GUIDE FOR THIS PLACE: 150 YEARS RETOLD © 2021 PORTAGE & MAIN PRESS ISBN: 978-1-77492-017-6

TEACHER GUIDE FOR THIS PLACE: 150 YEARS RETOLD © 2021 PORTAGE & MAIN PRESS ISBN-978-1-77492-017-6

	Lesson											
	1	2	3	4	5	6	7	8	9	10	11	12
3.3.2 Record Information Summarize and record information, ideas, and perspectives from a variety of sources; document sources accurately.			X	X	X	X	X	X	X	X	X	X
4.2.2. Revise Content Analyze and revise drafts to ensure appropriate content and to enhance unity, clarity, and coherence.			X	X	X	X			X	X	X	X
4.2.3 Enhance Legibility Use appropriate text features to enhance legibility for particular audiences, purposes, and contexts.			X		X	X			X	X	X	X
4.3.1 Grammar and Usage Select appropriate words, grammatical structures, and register for audience, purpose, and context.			X		X	X			X	X	X	X
4.3.2 Spelling Know and apply Canadian spelling conventions and monitor for correctness using appropriate resources; recognize adapted spellings for particular effects.			X		X	X			X	X	X	X
4.3.3 Capitalization and Punctuation Know and apply capitalization and punctuation conventions to clarify intended meaning, using appropriate resources as required.			X		X	X			X	X	X	X

	Lesson											
	1	2	3	4	5	6	7	8	9	10	11	12
4.4.2 Effective Oral and Visual Communication Use appropriate voice and visual production factors to communicate and emphasize intent in personal and public communication.		X		X	X			X	X	X	X	
5.1.1 Cooperate with Others Use language to build and maintain collaborative relationships; take responsibility for respectfully questioning others' viewpoints and requesting further explanation.		X		X	X			X	X	X	X	
5.1.2 Work in Groups Demonstrate flexibility in assuming a variety of group roles and take responsibility for tasks that achieve group goals.		X		X				X			X	
5.2.1. Compare Responses Identify various factors that shape understanding of texts, others, and self.		X		X				X	X		X	

TEACHER GUIDE FOR THIS PLACE: 150 YEARS RETOLD © 2021 PORTAGE & MAIN PRESS ISBN-978-1-77492-017-6

MANITOBA: GRADE 12 GLOBAL ISSUES: CITIZENSHIP AND SUSTAINABILITY

	Lesson											
	1	2	3	4	5	6	7	8	9	10	11	12
Curriculum Outcomes[16]												
Learning to Know *Acquire knowledge and understanding, and think critically about our complex and changing world.*												
Develop ecological literacy through an understanding of the interdependence of society, the environment, and the economy.			X					X	X			
Be open to new ideas and divergent thinking.		X	X	X	X	X	X	X	X	X	X	X
Seek knowledge from diverse sources and perspectives.		X			X			X	X	X		X
Conduct focused in-depth inquiry.		X			X			X	X	X		
Learning to Live Together *Learn to live peacefully with others and to care for our common homeland.*												
Engage in intercultural dialogue and cultivate a widening circle of empathy and concern.		X	X	X		X				X	X	
Be willing to collaborate, lead, and support.		X		X						X	X	
Enduring Understandings												
Our decisions and actions matter; they have social, environmental, economic, and political consequences.		X	X	X			X		X	X	X	X

TEACHER GUIDE FOR THIS PLACE: 150 YEARS RETOLD © 2021 PORTAGE & MAIN PRESS ISBN: 978-1-77492-017-6

16 Based on the 2017 edition of *Grade 12 Global Issues: Citizenship and Sustainability*.
https://www.edu.gov.mb.ca/k12/cur/socstud/global_issues/index.html

	Lesson											
	1	2	3	4	5	6	7	8	9	10	11	12
Individuals, groups, governments, and corporations have the power to effect change and the responsibility to contribute to a sustainable future.			X								X	
Indigenous knowledge and worldviews offer alternatives to prevailing assumptions about how to live with one another within the environment.		X	X	X	X	X	X	X	X	X	X	X
Political systems distribute power, privilege, and wealth in different ways, some more justly than others.			X	X		X				X		
Take Action												
Explore Indigenous perspectives to extend the boundaries of the familiar and to challenge assumptions and practices.		X	X	X	X	X	X	X	X	X	X	X
Area of Inquiry: Indigenous Peoples												
the legacy of colonialism, colonization, and decolonization		X	X	X	X	X	X	X	X	X	X	X
enculturation, assimilation, and cultural loss		X	X	X	X	X	X	X	X	X	X	X
impact of development and globalization on Indigenous peoples, cultural homogenization, disappearance of Indigenous peoples and cultures								X	X	X		X
preservation of traditional Indigenous cultures and languages			X			X	X	X	X	X	X	X
recognition of distinctive Indigenous worldviews and values			X	X		X	X	X	X	X	X	X

MANITOBA: GRADE 12 CURRENT TOPICS IN FIRST NATIONS, MÉTIS, AND INUIT STUDIES

	Lesson											
Curriculum Outcomes[17]	1	2	3	4	5	6	7	8	9	10	11	12
1.1 Learn about the colonialist history of Canada and the impact of colonization on First Nations, Métis, and Inuit peoples in Canada.		X	X	X	X	X	X	X	X	X		X
1.2 Explore Indigenous identity from the viewpoint of First Nations, Métis, and Inuit peoples.		X	X	X	X	X	X	X	X	X		X
1.3 Examine contemporary mainstream Canadian society's perception of Indigenous people as "the other."					X		X	X	X	X		
2.1 Investigate the historic, political, and economic practices of Indigenous peoples in Canada, before and after the arrival of Europeans.			X	X		X		X	X	X		X
2.2 Explore treaty-making between western First Nations and Canada beginning in 1871.		X	X	X	X	X		X	X	X	X	
2.3 Examine the historic and contemporary significance of the *Indian Act*, including the paradox that it is at once discriminatory and racist while it also preserves the sanctity of reserve lands.			X	X	X	X	X	X	X	X	X	

17 Based on the 2011 edition of *Grade 12 Current Topics in First Nations, Métis, and Inuit Studies: A Foundation for Implementation*.
https://www.edu.gov.mb.ca/k12/abedu/foundation_gr12/full_doc.pdf

TEACHER GUIDE FOR THIS PLACE: 150 YEARS RETOLD © 2021 PORTAGE & MAIN PRESS ISBN: 978-1-7492-017-6

	Lesson											
	1	2	3	4	5	6	7	8	9	10	11	12
2.4 Explore the history of the Métis from their origins in the fur trade, to the birth of the Métis Nation in Red River and the conflicts that characterized Métis resistance to threats against their economic, cultural, and political traditions.		X										
2.5 Explore the struggle by First Nations, Métis, and Inuit peoples in Canada to regain the self-determination that was stripped from them by colonialist policies and practices.		X										
3.3 Examine traditional Indigenous concepts and practices of justice, as well as the impact of colonization and the imposition of a western judicial model on First Nations, Métis, and Inuit peoples.				X				X	X	X		
3.4 Explore traditional and contemporary Indigenous economies and the impact of colonization.			X					X	X	X		
5.1 Work independently as individuals or with a partner or small group to create a project focusing on a theme relevant to contemporary Indigenous cultures.			X		X				X	X		

ONTARIO: GRADE 9 ENGLISH (ACADEMIC)

	Lesson											
	1	2	3	4	5	6	7	8	9	10	11	12
Curriculum Outcomes[18]												
Oral Communication **Speaking to Communicate** By the end of this course, students will:												
2.1 communicate orally for a few different purposes and audiences		X	X	X			X			X	X	
2.2 demonstrate an understanding of a few different interpersonal speaking strategies and adapt them to suit the purpose, situation, and audience, exhibiting sensitivity to cultural differences		X	X	X			X			X	X	
2.3 communicate in a clear, coherent manner for a few different purposes	X	X	X	X	X	X	X	X	X	X	X	X
2.5 identify a few different vocal strategies and use them selectively and with sensitivity to audience needs			X	X	X					X		
Reading and Literature Studies **Reading for Meaning** By the end of this course, students will:												
1.1 read student- and teacher-selected texts from diverse cultures and historical periods, identifying specific purposes for reading		X	X	X	X	X	X	X	X	X	X	X

---

18 Based on the 2007 edition of *The Ontario Curriculum, Grades 9 and 10: English*.
http://www.edu.gov.on.ca/eng/curriculum/secondary/english910currb.pdf

	Lesson											
	1	2	3	4	5	6	7	8	9	10	11	12
1.2 use several different reading comprehension strategies before, during, and after reading to understand both simple and complex texts	X	X	X	X	X	X	X	X	X	X	X	X
Reading and Literature Studies **Understanding Form and Style** By the end of this course, students will:												
2.1 identify several different characteristics of literary, informational, and graphic text forms and explain how they help communicate meaning	X											X
2.2 identify several different text features and explain how they help communicate meaning	X											X
Writing **Developing and Organizing Content** By the end of this course, students will:												
1.2 generate and focus ideas for potential writing tasks, using several different strategies and print, electronic, and other resources, as appropriate	X		X		X	X			X	X	X	X
1.3 locate and select information to support ideas for writing, using several different strategies and print, electronic, and other resources, as appropriate			X	X	X				X	X		X
1.4 identify, sort, and order main ideas and supporting details for writing tasks, using several different strategies and organizational patterns suited to the content and purpose for writing			X	X	X				X	X	X	X

TEACHER GUIDE FOR THIS PLACE: 150 YEARS RETOLD © 2021 PORTAGE & MAIN PRESS   ISBN-978-1-77492-017-6

	Lesson											
	1	2	3	4	5	6	7	8	9	10	11	12

Writing
Using Knowledge of Form and Style
By the end of this course, students will:

	1	2	3	4	5	6	7	8	9	10	11	12
2.4 write complete sentences that communicate their meaning clearly and accurately, varying sentence type, structure, and length for different purposes and making logical transitions between ideas	X	X	X	X	X	X	X	X	X	X	X	X
2.6 revise drafts to improve the content, organization, clarity, and style of their written work, using a variety of teacher-modelled strategies			X		X				X	X	X	X

Writing
Applying Knowledge of Conventions
By the end of this course, students will:

	1	2	3	4	5	6	7	8	9	10	11	12
3.1 use knowledge of spelling rules and patterns, several different types of resources, and appropriate strategies to spell familiar and new words correctly	X	X	X	X	X	X		X	X	X	X	X
3.3 use punctuation correctly to communicate their intended meaning	X	X	X	X	X	X		X	X	X	X	X
3.4 use grammar conventions correctly to communicate their intended meaning clearly	X	X	X	X	X	X		X	X	X	X	X
3.5 proofread and correct their writing, using guidelines developed with the teacher and peers	X	X	X	X	X	X		X	X	X	X	X

TEACHER GUIDE FOR THIS PLACE: 150 YEARS RETOLD © 2021 PORTAGE & MAIN PRESS ISBN: 978-1-77492-017-6

	Lesson											
	1	2	3	4	5	6	7	8	9	10	11	12
3.6 use several different presentation features, including print and script, fonts, graphics, and layout, to improve the clarity and coherence of their written work and to engage their audience					X					X		
3.7 produce pieces of published work to meet criteria identified by the teacher, based on the curriculum expectations			X						X		X	

TEACHER GUIDE FOR THIS PLACE: 150 YEARS RETOLD © 2021 PORTAGE & MAIN PRESS ISBN: 978-1-77492-017-6

ONTARIO: GRADE 10 ENGLISH (ACADEMIC)

							Lesson					
	1	2	3	4	5	6	7	8	9	10	11	12
Curriculum Outcomes[19]												
Oral Communication **Speaking to Communicate** By the end of this course, students will:												
2.1 communicate orally for a variety of purposes, using language appropriate for the intended audience		X	X	X			X			X	X	
2.2 demonstrate an understanding of a variety of interpersonal speaking strategies and adapt them to suit the purpose, situation, and audience, exhibiting sensitivity to cultural differences		X	X	X			X			X	X	
2.3 communicate in a clear, coherent manner, using a structure and style appropriate to the purpose, subject matter, and intended audience	X	X	X	X	X	X	X	X	X	X	X	
2.5 identify a variety of vocal strategies, including tone, pace, pitch, and volume, and use them appropriately and with sensitivity to audience needs and cultural differences			X	X	X					X		

TEACHER GUIDE FOR THIS PLACE: 150 YEARS RETOLD © 2021 PORTAGE & MAIN PRESS ISBN: 978-1-77492-017-6

19 Based on the 2007 edition of *The Ontario Curriculum, Grades 9 and 10: English.* http://www.edu.gov.on.ca/eng/curriculum/secondary/english910currb.pdf

TEACHER GUIDE FOR THIS PLACE: 150 YEARS RETOLD © 2021 PORTAGE & MAIN PRESS ISBN-978-1-77492-017-6

	Lesson											
	1	2	3	4	5	6	7	8	9	10	11	12
Reading and Literature Studies **Reading for Meaning** By the end of this course, students will:												
1.1 read a variety of student- and teacher-selected texts from diverse cultures and historical periods, identifying specific purposes for reading		X	X	X	X	X	X	X	X	X	X	X
1.2 select and use appropriate reading comprehension strategies before, during, and after reading to understand texts, including increasingly complex texts	X	X	X	X	X	X	X	X	X	X	X	X
Reading and Literature Studies **Understanding Form and Style** By the end of this course, students will:												
2.1 identify a variety of characteristics of literary, informational, and graphic text forms and explain how they help communicate meaning	X											
2.2 identify a variety of text features and explain how they help communicate meaning	X											
Writing **Developing and Organizing Content** By the end of this course, students will:												
1.2 generate, expand, explore, and focus ideas for potential writing tasks, using a variety of strategies and print, electronic, and other resources, as appropriate	X		X		X	X			X	X	X	X

	Lesson											
	1	**2**	**3**	**4**	**5**	**6**	**7**	**8**	**9**	**10**	**11**	**12**
1.3 locate and select information to appropriately support ideas for writing, using a variety of strategies and print, electronic, and other resources, as appropriate			X	X	X				X	X		X
1.4 identify, sort, and order main ideas and supporting details for writing tasks, using a variety of strategies and organizational patterns suited to the content and the purpose for writing			X	X	X				X	X	X	X

Writing
Using Knowledge of Form and Style
By the end of this course, students will:

	Lesson											
2.4 write complete sentences that communicate their meaning clearly and accurately, varying sentence type, structure, and length to suit different purposes and making smooth and logical transitions between ideas	X	X	X	X	X	X	X	X	X	X	X	X
2.6 revise drafts to improve the content, organization, clarity, and style of their written work, using a variety of teacher-modelled strategies			X		X				X	X	X	X

Writing
Applying Knowledge of Conventions
By the end of this course, students will:

	Lesson											
3.1 use knowledge of spelling rules and patterns, a variety of resources, and appropriate strategies to recognize and correct their own and others' spelling errors	X	X	X	X	X	X		X	X	X	X	X

TEACHER GUIDE FOR THIS PLACE: 150 YEARS RETOLD © 2021 PORTAGE & MAIN PRESS ISBN: 978-1-77492-017-6

	Lesson											
	1	2	3	4	5	6	7	8	9	10	11	12
3.3 use punctuation correctly and appropriately to communicate their intended meaning	X	X	X	X	X	X		X	X	X	X	X
3.4 use grammar conventions correctly and appropriately to communicate their intended meaning clearly and fluently	X	X	X	X	X	X		X	X	X	X	X
3.5 proofread and correct their writing, using guidelines developed with the teacher and peers	X		X		X	X			X	X	X	X
3.6 use a variety of presentation features, including print and script, fonts, graphics, and layout, to improve the clarity and coherence of their work and to heighten its appeal for their audience					X					X		
3.7 produce pieces of published work to meet criteria identified by the teacher, based on the curriculum expectations			X						X		X	

ONTARIO: GRADE 10 FIRST NATIONS, MÉTIS, AND INUIT IN CANADA

	Lesson											
	1	2	3	4	5	6	7	8	9	10	11	12
Curriculum Outcomes[20]												
Historical Inquiry and Skill Development **A1. Historical Inquiry** Throughout this course, students will:												
A1.1 use appropriate terminology in their investigations when referring to Indigenous peoples, nations, traditional territories, customs, traditions, and artefacts in Canada	X	X	X	X	X	X	X	X	X	X	X	
A1.3 formulate different types of questions to guide investigations into issues, events, and/or developments in the history of Indigenous peoples in Canada from pre-Contact to the present day		X							X	X		X
A1.5 assess the credibility of sources and information relevant to their investigations while respecting Indigenous worldviews and ways of knowing		X	X	X	X	X	X	X	X	X		
A1.9 communicate their ideas, arguments, and conclusions using various formats and styles, as appropriate for the audience and purpose	X	X	X	X	X	X	X	X	X	X	X	X

20 Based on the 2019 edition of *The Ontario Curriculum, Grades 9 to 12: First Nations, Métis and Inuit Studies.*
http://www.edu.gov.on.ca/eng/curriculum/secondary/First-nations-metis-inuit-studies-grades-9-12.pdf

TEACHER GUIDE FOR THIS PLACE: 150 YEARS RETOLD © 2021 PORTAGE & MAIN PRESS ISBN: 978-1-77492-017-6

TEACHER GUIDE FOR THIS PLACE: 150 YEARS RETOLD © 2021 PORTAGE & MAIN PRESS ISBN: 978-1-77492-017-6

	Lesson											
	1	2	3	4	5	6	7	8	9	10	11	12
Historical Inquiry and Skill Development **A2. Developing Transferable Skills** Throughout this course, students will:												
A2.3 apply the knowledge and skills developed in the study of the history of Indigenous peoples in Canada when analyzing current social, economic, and/or political issues	X	X	X	X	X	X	X	X	X	X	X	X
1876-1969: Assimilation, Encroachment, and Life in the Industrial Age **E1. Social, Economic, and Political Context** By the end of this course, students will:												
E1.1 analyze the impact of the *Indian Act* on First Nations communities and individuals during this period	X	X	X	X	X	X	X	X	X			
E1.2 describe some key economic trends and developments that affected Indigenous peoples in Canada during this period, and analyze the impact on their lives	X	X		X	X	X	X	X	X			
1876-1969: Assimilation, Encroachment, and Life in the Industrial Age **E2. Communities, Conflict, and Cooperation** By the end of this course, students will:												
E2.3 analyze how attitudes towards Indigenous peoples in Canada during this period contributed to conflict and other challenges	X	X	X	X	X	X	X	X	X			X
E2.4 assess the significance of Indigenous contributions to wars in which Canada participated during this period					X							

	Lesson											
---	1	2	3	4	5	6	7	8	9	10	11	12
1876-1969: Assimilation, Encroachment, and Life in the Industrial Age **E3. Identities, Cultures, and Self-Determination** By the end of this course, students will:												
E3.1 analyze various short- and long-term consequences of Indian residential school policy and the practices associated with it							X					
E3.2 analyze strategies used by some individuals and groups during this period to secure the recognition of Aboriginal title and treaty rights, and/or respect for Indigenous identities, and assess the impact of these strategies		X	X		X		X	X	X	X		X
E3.3 describe some environmental issues that had an impact on Indigenous communities during this period, and explain their significance for Indigenous individuals and communities and some non-Indigenous groups in Canada										X		
1969 to the Present: Resilience, Determination, and Reconciliation **F1. Social, Economic, and Political Context** By the end of this course, students will:												
F1.1 explain how some social trends, movements, and developments have affected Indigenous individuals and communities in Canada during this period, including in interactions with non-Indigenous Canadians											X	

TEACHER GUIDE FOR THIS PLACE: 150 YEARS RETOLD © 2021 PORTAGE & MAIN PRESS ISBN: 978-1-77492-017-6

	Lesson											
	1	2	3	4	5	6	7	8	9	10	11	12
F1.2 describe some key economic trends and developments that have affected Indigenous individuals and communities in Canada during this period, and analyze the impact on their lives									X			
F1.3 describe some key political trends and developments that have affected Indigenous individuals and communities in Canada during this period, and analyze the impact on their lives										X		
1969 to the Present: Resilience, Determination, and Reconciliation **F2. Communities, Conflict, and Cooperation** By the end of this course, students will:												
F2.5 describe some major instances of conflict involving Indigenous peoples in Canada during this period, and analyze some of their causes and consequences										X		
1969 to the Present: Resilience, Determination, and Reconciliation **F3. Identities, Cultures, and Self-Determination** By the end of this course, students will:												
F3.2 analyze the contributions of some individuals and groups to efforts to raise awareness about sovereignty/self-governance and to gain recognition of Aboriginal title and/or treaty rights during this period		X	X		X			X	X	X		

ONTARIO: GRADE 11 ENGLISH (UNIVERSITY PREPARATION)

						Lesson						
	1	**2**	**3**	**4**	**5**	**6**	**7**	**8**	**9**	**10**	**11**	**12**
Curriculum Outcomes[21]												
Oral Communication **Speaking to Communicate** By the end of this course, students will:												
2.1 communicate orally for a range of purposes, using language appropriate for the intended audience		X	X	X				X			X	X	
2.2 demonstrate an understanding of a variety of interpersonal speaking strategies and adapt them to suit the purpose, situation, and audience, exhibiting sensitivity to cultural differences		X	X	X				X			X	X	
2.3 communicate in a clear, coherent manner, using a structure and style effective for the purpose, subject matter, and intended audience	X	X	X	X	X	X	X	X	X	X	X	
2.5 identify a variety of vocal strategies, including tone, pace, pitch, and volume, and use them effectively and with sensitivity to audience needs and cultural differences			X	X	X					X		

TEACHER GUIDE FOR THIS PLACE: 150 YEARS RETOLD © 2021 PORTAGE & MAIN PRESS ISBN: 978-1-77492-017-6

---

21 Based on the 2007 edition of *The Ontario Curriculum, Grades 11 and 12: English*.
http://www.edu.gov.on.ca/eng/curriculum/secondary/english1112currb.pdf

TEACHER GUIDE FOR THIS PLACE: 150 YEARS RETOLD © 2021 PORTAGE & MAIN PRESS ISBN: 978-1-77492-017-6

	Lesson											
	1	2	3	4	5	6	7	8	9	10	11	12
Reading and Literature Studies **Reading for Meaning** By the end of this course, students will:												
1.1 read a variety of student- and teacher-selected texts from diverse cultures and historical periods, identifying specific purposes for reading		X	X	X	X	X	X	X	X	X	X	X
1.2 select and use appropriate reading comprehension strategies before, during, and after reading to understand texts, including increasingly complex texts	X	X	X	X	X	X	X	X	X	X	X	X
Reading and Literature Studies **Understanding Form and Style** By the end of this course, students will:												
2.1 identify a variety of characteristics of literary, informational, and graphic text forms and explain how they help communicate meaning	X											X
2.2 identify a variety of text features and explain how they help communicate meaning	X											X
Writing **Developing and Organizing Content** By the end of this course, students will:												
1.2 generate, expand, explore, and focus ideas for potential writing tasks, using a variety of strategies and print, electronic, and other resources, as appropriate	X		X		X	X			X	X	X	X

	Lesson											
	1	2	3	4	5	6	7	8	9	10	11	12
1.3 locate and select information to effectively support ideas for writing, using a variety of strategies and print, electronic, and other resources, as appropriate			X	X	X				X	X		X
1.4 identify, sort, and order main ideas and supporting details for writing tasks, using a variety of strategies and selecting the organizational pattern best suited to the content and the purpose for writing			X	X	X				X	X	X	X
Writing **Using Knowledge of Form and Style** By the end of this course, students will:												
2.4 write complete sentences that communicate their meaning clearly and effectively, varying sentence type, structure, and length to suit different purposes and making smooth and logical transitions between ideas	X	X	X	X	X	X	X	X	X	X	X	X
2.6 revise drafts to improve the content, organization, clarity, and style of their written work, using a variety of teacher-modelled strategies			X		X				X	X	X	X
Writing **Applying Knowledge of Conventions** By the end of this course, students will:												
3.1 use knowledge of spelling rules and patterns, a variety of resources, and appropriate strategies to recognize and correct their own and others' spelling errors	X	X	X	X	X	X		X	X	X	X	X

TEACHER GUIDE FOR THIS PLACE: 150 YEARS RETOLD © 2021 PORTAGE & MAIN PRESS ISBN: 978-1-77492-017-6

TEACHER GUIDE FOR THIS PLACE: 150 YEARS RETOLD © 2021 PORTAGE & MAIN PRESS ISBN: 978-1-77492-017-6

	Lesson											
	1	2	3	4	5	6	7	8	9	10	11	12
3.3 use punctuation correctly and appropriately to communicate their intended meaning	X	X	X	X	X	X		X	X	X	X	X
3.4 use grammar conventions correctly and appropriately to communicate their intended meaning clearly and fluently	X	X	X	X	X	X		X	X	X	X	X
3.5 regularly proofread and correct their writing			X		X				X	X	X	X
3.6 use a variety of presentation features, including print and script, fonts, graphics, and layout, to improve the clarity and coherence of their work and to heighten its appeal for their audience					X					X		
3.7 produce pieces of published work to meet criteria identified by the teacher, based on the curriculum expectations			X						X			

ONTARIO: GRADE 11 ENGLISH: UNDERSTANDING CONTEMPORARY FIRST NATIONS, MÉTIS, AND INUIT VOICES (UNIVERSITY PREPARATION)

	Lesson											
	1	2	3	4	5	6	7	8	9	10	11	12
Curriculum Outcomes[22]												
First Nations, Métis, and Inuit Perspectives and Text Forms in Canada **A1. Exploring** Throughout this course, students will:												
A1.3 identify and explain diverse themes, ideas, and issues related to First Nations, Métis, and Inuit identities, as reflected in various Indigenous text forms, and, as appropriate, in relevant non-Indigenous texts		X	X	X	X	X	X	X	X	X	X	X
A1.4 identify and explain diverse themes, ideas, and issues associated with relationships in First Nations, Métis, and Inuit cultures, as reflected in various Indigenous text forms, and, as appropriate, in relevant non-Indigenous texts		X	X	X	X	X	X	X	X	X	X	X
A1.5 identify and explain diverse themes, ideas, and issues related to First Nations, Métis, and Inuit self-determination, sovereignty, or self governance, as reflected in various Indigenous text forms, and, as appropriate, in relevant non-Indigenous texts		X	X	X	X	X	X	X	X	X	X	X

TEACHER GUIDE FOR THIS PLACE: 150 YEARS RETOLD © 2021 PORTAGE & MAIN PRESS ISBN-978-1-77492-017-6

---

22 Based on the 2019 edition of *The Ontario Curriculum, Grades 9 to 12: First Nations, Métis and Inuit Studies.*
http://www.edu.gov.on.ca/eng/curriculum/secondary/First-nations-metis-inuit-studies-grades-9-12.pdf

	Lesson											
	1	2	3	4	5	6	7	8	9	10	11	12
First Nations, Métis, and Inuit Perspectives and Text Forms in Canada **A2. Deconstructing** Throughout this course, students will:												
A2.5 describe a range of issues related to attempts to apply Western cultural criteria to First Nations, Métis, and Inuit text forms, including cultural text forms	X	X	X	X	X	X	X	X	X	X	X	X
First Nations, Métis, and Inuit Perspectives and Text Forms in Canada **A3. Reconstructing** Throughout this course, students will:												
A3.1 demonstrate an understanding of the challenges First Nations, Métis, and Inuit individuals and communities face and have faced in controlling their own narratives and resisting colonialist views, as revealed in text forms studied in this course	X	X	X	X	X	X	X	X	X	X	X	X
A3.5 describe various contemporary efforts to affirm the value and counteract the under-valuation of First Nations, Métis, and Inuit cultural text forms	X	X	X	X	X	X	X	X	X	X	X	X
Oral Communication **B1. The Oral Tradition** Throughout this course, students will:												
B1.1 identify various text forms associated with the oral traditions of First Nations, Métis, and Inuit cultures; explain their purpose and symbolic meaning; and describe various customs governing their use	X	X	X	X	X	X	X	X	X	X	X	X

	Lesson											
	1	2	3	4	5	6	7	8	9	10	11	12
B1.2 describe a variety of significant figures from First Nations, Métis, and Inuit oral stories including their origins, roles, characteristics, and behavior, and explain, with increasing insight, how they reflect a particular culture's worldview		X	X		X			X	X	X		
B1.4 select and use culturally appropriate listening practices during oral teachings by First Nations, Métis, and Inuit speakers	X	X	X	X	X	X	X	X	X	X	X	X

Oral Communication
B3. Speaking to Communicate
Throughout this course, students will:

	1	2	3	4	5	6	7	8	9	10	11	12
B3.1 orally communicate information and ideas related to First Nations, Métis, and Inuit cultures and/or perspectives for a range of purposes, using language and following social codes appropriate for the intended purpose and audience		X	X	X	X	X	X			X	X	
B3.2 demonstrate an understanding of a variety of interpersonal speaking strategies, and adapt them effectively to suit the purpose, situation, and audience, exhibiting sensitivity to cultural differences		X	X	X	X	X	X			X	X	

	Lesson											
	1	2	3	4	5	6	7	8	9	10	11	
B3.3 orally communicate information and ideas related to First Nations, Métis, and Inuit cultures and/or perspectives in a clear, coherent manner, using a structure and style effective for the purpose, subject matter, and intended audience		X	X	X	X	X	X			X	X	
B3.7 use a variety of audio-visual aids effectively to support and enhance oral presentations on subject matter related to First Nations, Métis, and Inuit cultures, and to engage their intended audience					X					X		

Reading and Literature Studies
C1. Reading for Meaning
Throughout this course, students will:

	Lesson											
	1	2	3	4	5	6	7	8	9	10	11	
C1.1 read a variety of student- and teacher-selected contemporary texts from diverse First Nations, Métis, and Inuit cultures, and, as appropriate, relevant texts from non-Indigenous sources and historical texts, identifying specific purposes for reading		X	X	X	X	X	X	X	X	X	X	X
C1.2 select and use the most appropriate reading comprehension strategies before, during, and after reading to understand texts from First Nations, Métis, and Inuit cultures, and, as appropriate, relevant texts from non-Indigenous sources, including increasingly complex or difficult texts		X	X	X	X	X	X	X	X	X	X	X

	Lesson											
	1	2	3	4	5	6	7	8	9	10	11	12
C1.5 extend their understanding of texts from First Nations, Métis, and Inuit cultures, and, as appropriate, relevant texts from non-Indigenous sources, including increasingly complex or difficult texts, by making rich connections between the ideas in them and in other texts and to their own knowledge, experience, and insights		X	X	X	X	X	X	X	X	X	X	X
Reading and Literature Studies **C2. Understanding Form and Style** Throughout this course, students will:												
C2.1 identify a variety of characteristics of literary, informational, and graphic text forms, and explain, with increasing insight, how they help communicate meaning or reflect a worldview	X											X
Writing **D1. Developing and Organizing Content** Throughout this course, students will:												
D1.2 generate, expand, explore, and focus ideas for potential writing tasks, using a variety of strategies and print, electronic, and other resources, as appropriate and with increasing effectiveness	X	X	X	X	X	X	X	X	X	X	X	X
D1.3 locate and select information to effectively support ideas for writing, using a variety of strategies and print, electronic, and other resources, as appropriate	X	X	X	X	X	X		X	X	X	X	X

TEACHER GUIDE FOR THIS PLACE: 150 YEARS RETOLD © 2021 PORTAGE & MAIN PRESS ISBN: 978-1-77492-017-6

	Lesson											
	1	2	3	4	5	6	7	8	9	10	11	12
D1.4 identify, sort, and order main ideas and supporting details for writing tasks, using a variety of strategies and selecting the organizational pattern best suited to the content and the purpose for writing	X	X	X	X	X	X		X	X	X	X	X
D1.5 determine whether the ideas and information gathered are accurate and complete, interesting, and effectively meet the requirements of the writing task	X	X	X	X	X	X			X	X	X	X

Writing
D2. Using Knowledge of Form and Style
Throughout this course, students will:

	1	2	3	4	5	6	7	8	9	10	11	12
D2.4 write complete sentences that communicate their meaning clearly and effectively, skillfully varying sentence type, structure, and length to suit different purposes and making smooth and logical transitions between ideas	X	X	X	X	X	X		X	X	X	X	X
D2.6 revise drafts to improve the content, organization, clarity, and style of their written work, using a variety of teacher-modelled strategies with increasing effectiveness	X	X	X	X	X	X			X	X	X	X

TEACHER GUIDE FOR THIS PLACE: 150 YEARS RETOLD © 2021 PORTAGE & MAIN PRESS ISBN: 978-1-77492-017-6

	Lesson											
	1	2	3	4	5	6	7	8	9	10	11	12
Writing **D3. Applying Knowledge of Conventions** Throughout this course, students will:												
D3.1 consistently use knowledge of spelling rules and patterns, a variety of resources, and appropriate strategies to identify and correct their own and others' spelling errors	X	X	X	X	X	X		X	X	X	X	X
D3.3 use punctuation correctly and effectively to communicate their intended meaning	X	X	X	X	X	X		X	X	X	X	X
D3.4 use grammar conventions correctly and appropriately to communicate their intended meaning clearly and effectively	X	X	X	X	X	X		X	X	X	X	X
D3.5 regularly proofread and correct their writing	X	X	X	X	X	X			X	X	X	X
D3.6 use a variety of presentation features, including print and script, fonts, graphics, and layout, to improve the clarity and coherence of their written work and to heighten its appeal and effectiveness for their audience					X					X		
D3.7 produce pieces of published work to meet criteria identified by the teacher, based on the curriculum expectations and respecting First Nations, Métis, and Inuit communication styles			X						X	X		

ONTARIO: GRADE 11 CONTEMPORARY FIRST NATIONS, MÉTIS, AND INUIT ISSUES AND PERSPECTIVES (UNIVERSITY/COLLEGE PREPARATION)

	Lesson											
	1	2	3	4	5	6	7	8	9	10	11	12
Curriculum Outcomes[23]												
Political Inquiry and Skill Development **A1. Political Inquiry** Throughout this course, students will:												
A1.2 select and organize relevant evidence, data, and information on contemporary issues, events, and/or developments relating to Indigenous peoples in Canada from a variety of primary and secondary sources, including Indigenous knowledge sources			X						X	X		X
A1.4 interpret and analyze evidence, data, and information relevant to their investigations, using various tools, strategies, and approaches appropriate for political inquiry			X						X	X		X
A1.7 communicate their ideas, arguments, and conclusions using various formats and styles, as appropriate for the audience and purpose	X	X	X	X	X		X	X	X	X	X

TEACHER GUIDE FOR THIS PLACE: 150 YEARS RETOLD © 2021 PORTAGE & MAIN PRESS ISBN: 978-1-77492-017-6

23 Based on the 2019 edition of *The Ontario Curriculum, Grades 9 to 12: First Nations, Métis and Inuit Studies*.
http://www.edu.gov.on.ca/eng/curriculum/secondary/First-nations-metis-inuit-studies-grades-9-12.pdf

	Lesson											
	1	2	3	4	5	6	7	8	9	10	11	12
Political Inquiry and Skill Development **A2. Developing Transferable Skills** Throughout this course, students will:												
A2.2 demonstrate in everyday contexts attributes, skills, and work habits developed through investigations into contemporary First Nations, Métis, and Inuit realities and perspectives		X	X	X	X	X	X	X	X	X	X	X
Cultural Identity and Cultural Continuity **B2. Cultural Revitalization and Cultural Continuity** Throughout this course, students will:												
B2.1 describe various ways in which First Nations, Métis, and Inuit communities are utilizing Indigenous knowledge sources to promote cultural revitalization and/or cultural continuity		X	X	X	X	X	X	X	X	X	X	X
B2.4 analyze the role of cultural observances/festivals and traditional knowledge practices in promoting First Nations, Métis, and Inuit cultural revitalization and/or cultural continuity			X									
Cultural Identity and Cultural Continuity **B3. Cultural Understanding and Cultural Leadership** Throughout this course, students will:												
B3.2 make inferences about the ways in which various forms of racism and cultural stereotyping have affected and continue to affect First Nations, Métis, and Inuit individuals and communities, drawing on political, social, and/or economic evidence to support their conclusions		X	X	X	X	X	X	X	X	X	X	X

	Lesson											
	1	2	3	4	5	6	7	8	9	10	11	12
B3.4 identify some significant First Nations, Métis, and Inuit leaders, artists, Elders, historians, and/or authors		X	X		X			X	X	X		

Community Perspectives
C1. Community Governance, Planning, and Administration
By the end of this course, students will:

	1	2	3	4	5	6	7	8	9	10	11	12
C1.2 identify and explain the significance of various contemporary economic issues and/or developments relating to First Nations, Métis, and Inuit community-planning initiatives									X			
C2.3 suggest a variety of ways in which effective leadership can contribute to the realization of First Nations, Métis, and Inuit community aspirations, drawing on evidence from communities in different regions of Canada			X									

National and Regional Perspectives
D3. National and Regional Leadership
Throughout this course, students will:

	1	2	3	4	5	6	7	8	9	10	11	12
D3.2 identify and describe various events and/or strategies that demonstrate the ability of First Nations, Métis, and Inuit leaders to influence public awareness of Indigenous realities in Canada							X		X	X		X

TEACHER GUIDE FOR THIS PLACE: 150 YEARS RETOLD © 2021 PORTAGE & MAIN PRESS ISBN-978-1-77492-017-6

ONTARIO: GRADE 12 ENGLISH (UNIVERSITY PREPARATION)

	Lesson											
	1	2	3	4	5	6	7	8	9	10	11	12
Curriculum Outcomes[24]												
Oral Communication **Speaking to Communicate** By the end of this course, students will:												
2.1 communicate orally for a wide range of purposes, using language effective for the intended audience		X	X	X			X			X	X	
2.2 demonstrate an understanding of a variety of interpersonal speaking strategies and adapt them to suit the purpose, situation, and audience, exhibiting sensitivity to cultural differences		X	X	X			X			X	X	
2.3 communicate in a clear, coherent manner, using a structure and style effective for the purpose, subject matter, and intended audience	X	X	X	X	X	X	X	X	X	X	X	
2.5 identify a variety of vocal strategies, including tone, pace, pitch, and volume, and use them effectively and with sensitivity to audience needs and cultural differences			X	X	X					X		

TEACHER GUIDE FOR THIS PLACE: 150 YEARS RETOLD © 2021 PORTAGE & MAIN PRESS ISBN: 978-1-77492-017-6

24 Based on the 2007 edition of *The Ontario Curriculum, Grades 11 and 12: English.*
   http://www.edu.gov.on.ca/eng/curriculum/secondary/english1112currb.pdf

	Lesson											
	1	2	3	4	5	6	7	8	9	10	11	12
Reading and Literature Studies **Reading for Meaning** By the end of this course, students will:												
1.1 read a variety of student- and teacher-selected texts from diverse cultures and historical periods, identifying specific purposes for reading		X	X	X	X	X	X	X	X	X	X	X
1.2 select and use, with increasing facility, the most appropriate reading comprehension strategies to understand texts, including complex and challenging texts	X	X	X	X	X	X	X	X	X	X	X	X
Reading and Literature Studies **Understanding Form and Style** By the end of this course, students will:												
2.1 identify a variety of characteristics of literary, informational, and graphic text forms and demonstrate insight into the way they help communicate meaning	X											X
2.2 identify a variety of text features and demonstrate insight into the way they communicate meaning	X											X
Writing **Developing and Organizing Content** By the end of this course, students will:												
1.2 generate, expand, explore, and focus ideas for potential writing tasks, using a variety of strategies and print, electronic, and other resources, as appropriate	X		X		X	X			X	X	X	X

TEACHER GUIDE FOR THIS PLACE: 150 YEARS RETOLD © 2021 PORTAGE & MAIN PRESS ISBN: 978-1-77492-017-6

	Lesson											
	1	2	3	4	5	6	7	8	9	10	11	12
1.3 locate and select information to fully and effectively support ideas for writing, using a variety of strategies and print, electronic, and other resources, as appropriate			X	X	X				X	X		X
1.4 identify, sort, and order main ideas and supporting details for writing tasks, using a variety of strategies and selecting the organizational pattern best suited to the content and the purpose for writing			X	X	X				X	X	X	X
Writing **Using Knowledge of Form and Style** By the end of this course, students will:												
2.4 write complete sentences that communicate their meaning clearly and effectively, skillfully varying sentence type, structure, and length to suit different purposes and making smooth and logical transitions between ideas	X	X	X	X	X	X	X	X	X	X	X	X
2.6 revise drafts to improve the content, organization, clarity, and style of their written work			X		X				X	X	X	X
Writing **Applying Knowledge of Conventions** By the end of this course, students will:												
3.1 use knowledge of spelling rules and patterns, a variety of resources, and appropriate strategies to recognize and correct their own and others' spelling errors	X	X	X	X	X	X		X	X	X	X	X

	Lesson											
	1	2	3	4	5	6	7	8	9	10	11	12
3.3 use punctuation correctly and effectively to communicate their intended meaning	X	X	X	X	X	X		X	X	X	X	X
3.4 use grammar conventions correctly and appropriately to communicate their intended meaning clearly and effectively	X	X	X	X	X	X		X	X	X	X	X
3.5 regularly proofread and correct their writing	X		X		X	X			X	X	X	X
3.6 use a variety of presentation features, including print and script, fonts, graphics, and layout, to improve the clarity and coherence of their written work and to heighten its appeal and effectiveness for their audience					X					X		
3.7 produce pieces of published work to meet criteria identified by the teacher, based on the curriculum expectations			X						X		X	

TEACHER GUIDE FOR THIS PLACE: 150 YEARS RETOLD © 2021 PORTAGE & MAIN PRESS ISBN: 978-1-77492-017-6

HOW DO WE READ GRAPHIC NOVELS? (ALL STORIES)

DURATION

One hour

OVERVIEW

Graphic novels (and comics) are a unique format of literature that include many parts. This lesson is designed to introduce teachers and students alike to the unique features of this format. Throughout the lesson, students will research the parts of a graphic novel and then create their own graphic novel scene incorporating these parts.

BACKGROUND

The terms *graphic novel* and *comic book* describe the format of a book, rather than a genre. Graphic novels and comic books can be fiction, non-fiction, biography, fantasy, dystopia, or any genre in between.[25] Graphic novels are an accessible reading resource for all students, and they have been proven to engage even the most reluctant of readers.[26] Graphic novels also include dialogue, characters' thoughts, narration, and captions. Graphic novels are meant to be read from left to right and top to bottom.

---

25 "What is a Graphic Novel?" Get Graphic, the Buffalo and Erie County Public Library and Partnering Organizations, accessed April 20, 2020, https://www.buffalolib.org/get-graphic/what-graphic-novel

26 Knutson, Sarah. "How Graphic Novels Help Students Develop Critical Skills," Room 241: A Blog by Concordia University-Portland, updated October 23, 2018, https://education.cu-portland.edu/blog/classroom-resources/graphic-novels-visual-literacy/.

TEACHER GUIDE FOR THIS PLACE: 150 YEARS RETOLD © 2021 PORTAGE & MAIN PRESS ISBN: 978-1-77492-017-6

MATERIALS

- whiteboard or chart paper
- markers
- Activity Sheet: All About Graphic Novels (1.1) (one copy for each student)
- Rubric: Graphic Novel Scene (1.2) (two copies for each student)
- pencil crayons
- art paper (one sheet for each student)
- computers/tablets with internet access (optional)
- writing utensils

ACTIVATE: BRAINSTORM

Ask students what graphic novels or comic books they have read. Make a list of these titles on a whiteboard or a sheet of chart paper. Then, work with students to create a list of the parts of a comic with which students are already familiar (e.g., captions, sound effects, thought balloons).

ACQUIRE: FILL IN THE ACTIVITY SHEET: ALL ABOUT GRAPHIC NOVELS

Give each student a copy of the Activity Sheet: All About Graphic Novels (1.1). Use the answer key below to read through the worksheet with the class. As you read the worksheet, have students fill in the missing words. Another option is to have students research and record the missing words as a "scavenger hunt" activity using online and print sources.

Alternatively, have students create their own template to record the parts of a graphic novel.

Answer Key for Activity Sheet: All About Graphic Novels (1.1):

(1) gutters

(2) a visual or implied boundary, and the contents within it, that tell a piece of the story

(3) the space between the panels; as the reader moves from one panel to the next, they predict and conclude what is happening

(4) gutters

(5) change

(6) description

(7) focus on a character's thoughts and ideas

(8) focus on conversation between characters

(9) use font and illustration to convey sound in a story

(10) dialogue

(11) narration

(12) motion

(13) moving

(14) realistic

(15) expressions

TEACHER GUIDE FOR THIS PLACE: 150 YEARS RETOLD © 2021 PORTAGE & MAIN PRESS ISBN-978-1-77492-017-6

APPLY: CREATE YOUR OWN GRAPHIC NOVEL SCENE

Explain to students that they will now create their own graphic novel scene. The scene can be an event from their day, such as their commute to school or an after-school activity.

Before they begin, ask students what they think should be included in the rubric that will be used to grade their assignment. Co-construct a rubric with the class. Alternatively, use the Rubric: Graphic Novel Scene (1.2).

Have students plan out their scenes by writing a brief description for each panel of the scene they would like to draw. Once they have each of their scenes planned (e.g., panel one: wake up in bed, panel two: brush teeth, panel three: eat breakfast, panel four: walk to school), students should write the dialogue, thoughts, and other elements they want to include. Students should aim to incorporate at least four of the different parts of a graphic novel discussed in the Acquire activity. Have each student fold a sheet of paper in half and in half again, so they have four panels (boxes) on each side to use for their graphic novel scene. Based on their written descriptions, have students sketch a rough draft of their scene in the panels they have created.

ASSESS: PEER ASSESSMENT AND GRAPHIC NOVEL SCENE RUBRIC

Before students submit their graphic novel scenes, have them engage in a peer-editing session. As a fair way to distribute the graphic novel scenes, collect the scenes and hand them back out in a random order. The scene the students receive is the one they will peer edit. Hand out one copy of the Rubric: Graphic Novel Scene (1.2) or the co-constructed rubric to each student. Have students review their partner's scene several times, and circle the level of proficiency they would give the student. Make sure students write an explanation for the grade they gave each category, using the back of the rubric to jot down their comments and suggestions for improvement. Remind students that constructive criticism is not personal and should include both positive comments and comments that suggest in a friendly manner an area needing improvement.

Once students have finished giving feedback on their partner's scene, have them hand back the story to their partner along with the rubric and comments. Allow students time to revise their work before submitting the graphic novel scenes to you for final grading. Use the co-constructed rubric or Rubric: Graphic Novel Scene (1.2) to assess students' work.

TEACHER GUIDE FOR THIS PLACE: 150 YEARS RETOLD © 2021 PORTAGE & MAIN PRESS   ISBN: 978-1-77492-017-6

Date: _____   Name: _____

ALL ABOUT GRAPHIC NOVELS

When reading a graphic novel, it's important to understand all of the elements that make up a graphic novel. Fill in the blanks as instructed below.

Panels and_____(1)
Define the following terms.

Panel: _____

_____(2)

Gutter: _____

_____(3)

Fill in the blanks below to complete the sentences.

Consider the size and shape of panels. How do they fit together? Do they interrupt or overlap each other? Are there any images without panel borders at all? The spaces in between the panels—the _____(4)—indicate a _____(5): in how time is passing, in where you are, or at which character you're looking at or talking to. What do the gutters add to how you understand the story?

gutter→

Panels from "Peggy" in *This Place: 150 Years Retold*, written by David A. Robertson and illustrated by Natasha Donovan.

gutter →

TEACHER GUIDE FOR THIS PLACE: 150 YEARS RETOLD © 2021 PORTAGE & MAIN PRESS ISBN: 978-1-77492-017-6

1.1

ALL ABOUT GRAPHIC NOVELS

_____(6) AND WORD BALLOONS

Define the following terms.

Thought Balloon: _____

_____(7)

Dialogue Balloon: _____

_____(8)

Sound Effect Balloon: _____

_____(9)

Fill in the blanks below to complete the sentences.

Think about how the _____ (10) appears. Are the words different colours? Written with thicker or thinner lines? How would that sound? How about the silence when no one is speaking? Is there any _____ (11) or description (words in boxes, but not spoken)? How is that important to how the story unfolds?

SOUND EFFECTS AND _____ (12) LINES

Sounds set the scene, signal something off-scene, and add another layer to each story. Motion lines indicate how characters or objects are _____ (13). What sounds do you see? How are each of the sounds written—does the way it's written reflect what it actually sounds like? What gestures do you see?

Panels from "Peggy" in *This Place: 150 Years Retold*, written by David A. Robertson and illustrated by Natasha Donovan.

ART

Every creator has their own style. Is the art _____ (14)? Cartoony? What can you tell from the _____ (15) on faces? The gestures and movement of characters? The background and its details? If there is colour, how does that change over the course of a page? Each chapter?

TEACHER GUIDE FOR THIS PLACE: 150 YEARS RETOLD © 2021 PORTAGE & MAIN PRESS ISBN: 978-1-77492-017-6

1.1

Date: _____   Name: _____

GRAPHIC NOVEL SCENE

CATEGORY	Excellent	Good	Developing/Needs Improvement
Comic Story Structure /10	The story/summary is very well-organized. One idea or scene follows another in a logical sequence with clear transitions.	The story/summary is pretty well-organized. One idea or scene may seem out of place. Clear transitions are used.	The story/summary is hard to follow. The transitions are sometimes not clear.
Visual Appeal /10	Carefully chosen images help the reader understand the action and emotions in the story/summary.	Most of the images help the reader understand the story. One or two are unrelated or confusing.	Comic includes many images that do not relate to the story and confuse readers.
Grammar & Spelling (Conventions) /5	Writer makes no errors in grammar or spelling that distract the reader from the content in the graphic novel scene.	Writer makes a few errors in grammar or spelling that distract the reader from the content in the graphic novel scene.	Writer makes many errors in grammar or spelling that distract the reader from the content in the graphic novel scene.
Effort /5	Final product is completed and pride in one's work, proper time management, and adequate planning is evident.	Final product is short, and more effort could have been put into time management and/or adequate planning.	Final product is incomplete—pride in one's work, proper time management, and/or adequate planning is not evident.

Mark out of 30:

Comments:

TEACHER GUIDE FOR THIS PLACE: 150 YEARS RETOLD © 2021 PORTAGE & MAIN PRESS ISBN: 978-1-77492-017-6

1.2

WHAT IS RESISTANCE?
(ANNIE OF RED RIVER)

TEACHER GUIDE FOR THIS PLACE: 150 YEARS RETOLD © 2021 PORTAGE & MAIN PRESS ISBN-978-1-77492-017-6

DURATION

Two to three hours

OVERVIEW

Throughout this lesson, students will learn about a lesser-known act of Métis resistance that took place in 1869. Students will begin by co-constructing a word splash that includes any prior knowledge about Métis culture, history, and resistance. Students will then engage in small group discussions regarding themes of morality and resistance while being respectful listeners and gaining the confidence to share their personal opinions with peers.

BACKGROUND

The Métis are a distinct group of Indigenous people with a unique history, culture, language, and territory that includes parts of present-day Ontario, Manitoba, and Saskatchewan. The Métis Nation is comprised of descendants of people born of relations between First Nations and French or Scottish settlers.

Louis Riel was a Métis leader who commanded two resistances in western Canada in an attempt to preserve Métis rights and culture. Eventually, Louis Riel was tried, convicted, and hanged for treason in 1885. For many years after his death, Louis Riel was regarded as a traitor. However, today most Canadians, particularly the Métis, have reclaimed him as a heroic patriot, a founder of Manitoba, and a Father of Confederation.

MATERIALS

- copies of *This Place: 150 Years Retold* (one for each student)
- whiteboard or chart paper
- markers
- computers/tablets with internet access (optional)
- Activity Sheet: Historical Figure, Stages of Life (2.1) (one copy for each student) OR Activity Sheet: Historical Connections (2.2) (one copy for each student)
- Peer Assessment: Small Group Discussions (2.3) (one copy for each student)
- Rubric: Written Reflection (2.4) (one copy for each student)
- writing utensils

ACTIVATE: WORD SPLASH

Before beginning the lesson, inform the class that they will be learning about an event from Métis history. Create a word splash on the whiteboard or on chart paper and solicit student responses that include any prior knowledge students have about Métis identity, culture, history, and current topics. Begin by asking the class:

- What do you know about Métis culture and history?
- What do you know about Métis identity and current topics?

ACQUIRE: READ "ANNIE OF RED RIVER"

As a class, read the author's statement on pages 2–3 of *This Place: 150 Years Retold*, and the author's biography in the "About the Contributors" section, which begins on page 284 in the book.

Ask the class:

- Does anyone know what *cultural appropriation is*?
- What are some examples of cultural appropriation? (e.g., non-Indigenous designers copying traditional Indigenous designs for clothing and selling it for a profit)

Solicit responses. Next, explain that Canadian copyright law protects Indigenous knowledge, including traditional cultural expressions. This means that it is illegal to profit off of the culture of Indigenous peoples in Canada. However, there are some grey areas—for example, some oral stories may be difficult to protect. Discuss with students that it is generally considered wrong to profit off of a culture that is not your own.

Ask the class to consider the following question:

- What would make "Annie of Red River" an authentic Indigenous text?

Discuss with students that authentic texts present authentic Indigenous voices, depict themes

TEACHER GUIDE FOR THIS PLACE: 150 YEARS RETOLD © 2021 PORTAGE & MAIN PRESS ISBN-978-1-77492-017-6

and issues important to Indigenous peoples, and include respectful portrayals or representations of Indigenous peoples and their traditions and beliefs. In this case, the answer is yes because the author, Katherena Vermette, identifies as Métis and is writing about a significant event in Métis history.

Restate the importance of assessing the authenticity of texts to honour Indigenous voices and the right for Indigenous peoples to reclaim their own stories and histories.

Next, as a class, read the timeline that appears before "Annie of Red River" on pages 2–3 of *This Place: 150 Years Retold*. If students are not familiar with Louis Riel, have them briefly research the historical figure and record their notes on the Activity Sheet: Historical Figure, Stages of Life (2.1).

Alternatively, have students choose a historical event from the timeline, and briefly research the event and its significance to Canadian history. Have students use the Activity Sheet: Historical Connections (2.2) to organize their findings.

Before students individually read "Annie of Red River," show them a map of the Red River Métis Settlement in 1870, where Annie lived. The "Manitoba, Red River Settlement, 1870" map on the Gabriel Dumont Institute website is a good example (go to <http://www.metismuseum.ca/resource.php/01828>). Next, show students a map of the modern-day Exchange District, which is a booming downtown neighbourhood in Winnipeg, Manitoba at the same location. The Exchange District Biz has a map of the area on their website (go to <https://exchangedistrict.org/map/>).

APPLY: SMALL GROUP DISCUSSIONS

Once students have finished reading the story, randomly organize students into groups of four. Small groups will give all students a chance to speak in the discussion. Have each group sit in a circle.

Remind students that the goal is to engage in high-level discussions about the issues presented in the story and that their peers will be marking their participation. Review the importance of discussion etiquette, including being respectful to all group members, ensuring that all members have a chance to speak, and staying on topic.

Write the following questions on the whiteboard, and allow a minimum of five minutes of discussion for each question:

1. What were your initial thoughts after reading the story?
2. Why do you think this story was included in the anthology? What significance does this story hold?
3. Do you agree with Annie's actions? How would you have handled the situation?

TEACHER GUIDE FOR THIS PLACE: 150 YEARS RETOLD © 2021 PORTAGE & MAIN PRESS ISBN 978-1-77492-017-6

4. How does the graphic novel format influence readers' reactions to the text? Do you think readers would have the same reaction if the story was presented as a short story or novel?

5. What other types of resistance might be effective in creating change? Do you know of any other specific acts of Métis resistance?

Solicit whole-class responses after each question has been discussed. Have a volunteer from each group summarize what they discussed.

ASSESS: PEER ASSESSMENT AND WRITTEN REFLECTION RUBRIC

Once discussions have concluded, have students complete the Peer Assessment: Small Group Discussions (2.3). Next, have students write a one-page written reflection using the following prompt, which can be written on the whiteboard.

Respond thoughtfully and critically to the following prompt:

> *Please describe your experience engaging in the discussion. Were your viewpoints strengthened or challenged? What is one thing that another group member said that you agreed with? What is one thing that another group members said that you disagreed with? How would you rate your participation in the discussions? What would you do differently next time?*

Assess the students' reflections using the Rubric: Written Reflection (2.4).

TEACHER GUIDE FOR THIS PLACE: 150 YEARS RETOLD © 2021 PORTAGE & MAIN PRESS ISBN: 978-1-77492-017-6

Date: _____ Name: _____

HISTORICAL FIGURE, STAGES OF LIFE

Name of Historical Figure:_____

EARLY LIFE
Place of Birth
Family History

ADOLESCENCE
Childhood experiences

END OF LIFE
Death
Historical significance

ADULTHOOD
Accomplishments
Contributions
Interesting facts
about their life

TEACHER GUIDE FOR THIS PLACE: 150 YEARS RETOLD © 2021 PORTAGE & MAIN PRESS ISBN: 978-1-77492-017-6

Date: _____ Name: _____

HISTORICAL CONNECTIONS

Historical Event:_____

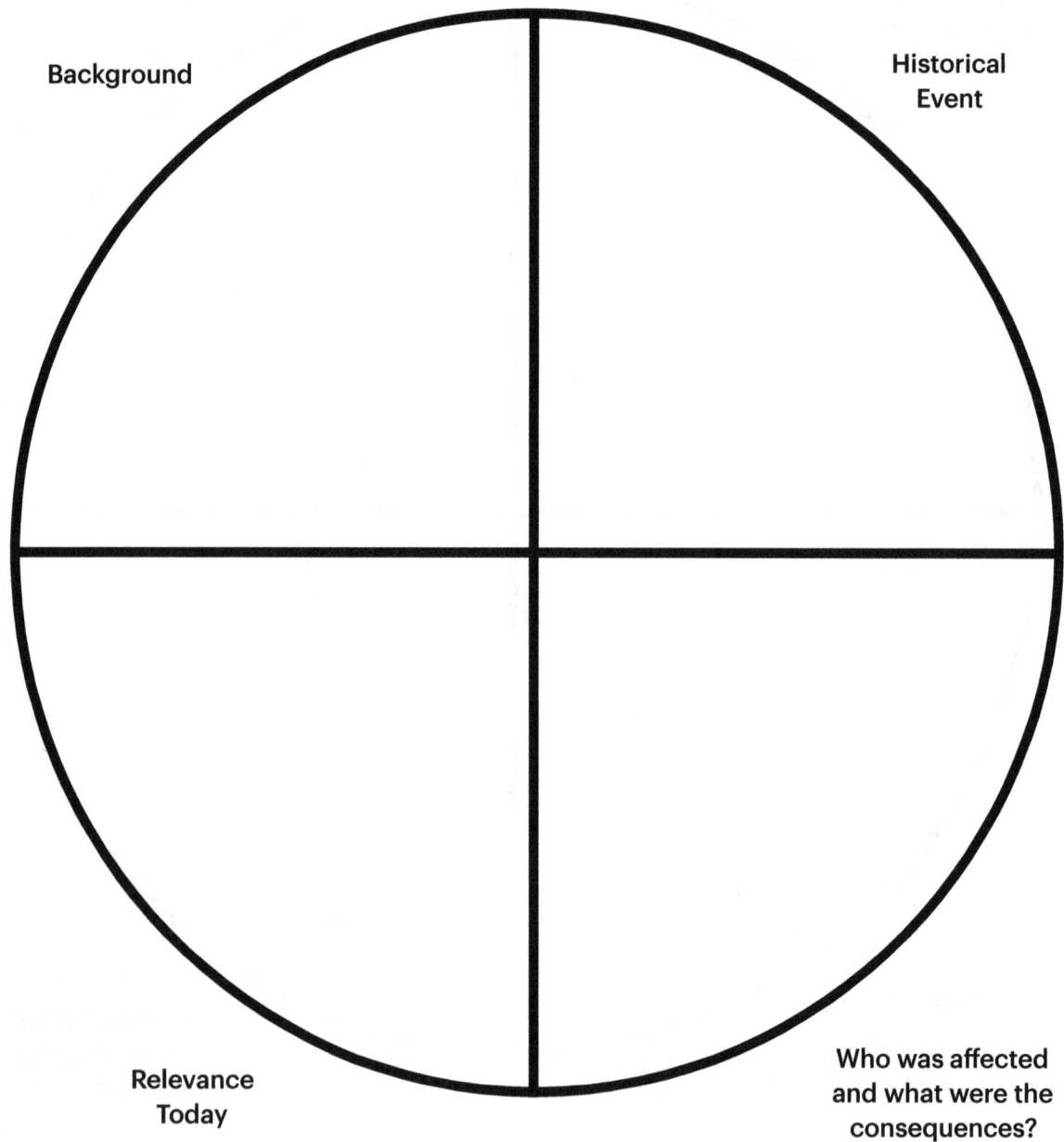

TEACHER GUIDE FOR THIS PLACE: 150 YEARS RETOLD © 2021 PORTAGE & MAIN PRESS   ISBN-978-1-77492-017-6

Background

Historical
Event

Relevance
Today

Who was affected
and what were the
consequences?

2.2

Date: _____   Name: _____

PEER ASSESSMENT: SMALL GROUP DISCUSSIONS

Please give each of your group members a mark out of three for each category of participation. Assess your own participation in the last column.

Group Members				My Self-Assessment
Contributed to the discussion				
Demonstrated respect for others' opinions				
Maintained attentiveness throughout the discussion				
Invited others to speak in the discussion				

TEACHER GUIDE FOR THIS PLACE: 150 YEARS RETOLD © 2021 PORTAGE & MAIN PRESS ISBN-978-1-77492-017-6

2.3

Date: _____   Name: _____

WRITTEN REFLECTION RUBRIC

CATEGORY	Excellent	Good	Developing/Needs Improvement
Depth of reflection /5	Writing demonstrates an in-depth reflection on topic. Supporting details and/or examples are clearly identified.	Writing demonstrates a general reflection on the topic, including some supporting details and examples.	Writing demonstrates a minimal reflection on the topic including a few supporting details and examples.
Required components /10	Writing surpasses the required components of the assignment.	Writing includes the required components of the assignment.	Writing includes a few of the required components of the assignment.
Structure & Organization /3	Writing is clear, concise, and well organized with the use of excellent sentence/paragraph structure. Thoughts are expressed in a logical manner.	Writing is mostly clear, concise, and organized with the use of good sentence/paragraph structure. Thoughts are expressed in a logical manner.	Writing is unclear, and thoughts are not well organized. Thoughts are not expressed in a logical manner.
Grammar /2	There are no spelling or grammar errors.	There are a few spelling or grammatical errors.	There are several spelling or grammatical errors.

Total out of 20 marks:

Comments:

TEACHER GUIDE FOR THIS PLACE: 150 YEARS RETOLD © 2021 PORTAGE & MAIN PRESS ISBN: 978-1-77492-017-6

WHAT MAKES A LEADER GREAT? (TILTED GROUND)

TEACHER GUIDE FOR THIS PLACE: 150 YEARS RETOLD © 2021 PORTAGE & MAIN PRESS ISBN-978-1-77492-017-6

DURATION

Two to four hours

OVERVIEW

Throughout this lesson, students will brainstorm qualities that make an effective leader and then read a story about outstanding Ligwitdaxw leader Chief Billy Assu. Students will choose a present-day leader to research and then write an essay comparing and contrasting their chosen leader to Chief Billy Assu.

BACKGROUND

British Columbia is home to 198 First Nations, each who have their own distinct cultures, histories, and traditions. BC has the greatest diversity of Indigenous cultures in Canada. Most BC First Nations did not sign treaties in the past, making the land of BC unceded territory. *Unceded territory* refers to land that First Nations have never legally signed away the rights to. At the time of publication, the Government of Canada and the Province of British Columbia are currently negotiating with 70 percent of BC First Nations through the BC Treaty Process.

What is a potlach? A potlach is a gift-sharing and feasting tradition practised by many Indigenous nations on the west coast of Canada. People who speak Kwak´wala, the Kwakwa̲ka'wakw, believe that a great leader is a person who gives the most away. Since a time beyond memory, the Kwakwa̲ka'wakw have been hosting potlatches, and potlatching continues to play a central and unifying role in community life today, including the important function of redistributing wealth among community members and guests. The potlatch ceremony marks important occasions in the lives of the Kwakwa̱ka'wakw including the naming of children, marriage, transferring rights and privileges, and mourning the dead.[27]

MATERIALS

- copies of *This Place: 150 Years Retold* (one for each student)
- computers/tablets with internet access (optional)
- Activity Sheet: Historical Connections from lesson 2 (2.2) (one copy for each student)
- Activity Sheet: Compare and Contrast Essay Outline (3.1) (one copy for each student)
- Rubric: Compare and Contrast Essay (3.2) (two copies for each student)
- writing utensils

ACTIVATE: THINK/PAIR/SHARE

Divide students into pairs. Have them discuss with their partner what it means to be a good leader and generate a list of the qualities of a good leader.

After a few minutes of discussion, have each group share their ideas with the rest of the class.

Before reading "Tilted Ground," invite an Elder from a Nation that practises the potlatch to talk about the ceremony with students. See Inviting an Elder Into Your Learning Space, on page 8, for guidelines for inviting an Elder to speak with students.

Alternatively, show the class the following videos on the importance of a potlach and the significance of the potlatch ban.

- \<https://www.youtube.com/watch?v=WvzqCbdyFIM\>
  "Potlatch 67-67: Why We Potlatch." Potlatch 67-67. (1:30).

In this video, Chief Rob Everson discusses why community members hold potlach ceremonies.

- \<https://www.youtube.com/watch?v=3IH6_j2R0C8\>
  "Potlatch 67-67: An Interview with Dr. Evelyn Voyageur." Potlatch 67-67. (31:12).

In this video, Elder Dr. Evelyn Voyageur discusses the importance of the potlatch and its connection to culture in her home community of Dzawada'enuxw First Nation, British Columbia.

---

27 "Potlatch." *Living Tradition, The Kwakwaka'wakw Potlatch on the Northwest Coast.* Accessed March 26, 2020. https://umistapotlatch.ca/potlatch-eng.php

TEACHER GUIDE FOR THIS PLACE: 150 YEARS RETOLD © 2021 PORTAGE & MAIN PRESS ISBN: 978-1-77492-017-6

ACQUIRE: READ "TILTED GROUND"

As a class, read the author's statement on pages 28–29 of *This Place: 150 Years Retold*, and the author's biography in the "About the Contributors" section, which begins on page 284 in the book.

Ask the class:

- Does anyone know what *cultural appropriation* is?
- What are some examples of cultural appropriation? (e.g., non-Indigenous designers copying traditional Indigenous designs for clothing and selling it for a profit)

Solicit responses. Next, explain that Canadian copyright law protects Indigenous knowledge, including traditional cultural expressions. This means that it is illegal to profit off of the culture of Indigenous peoples in Canada. However, there are some grey areas—for example, some oral stories may be difficult to protect. Discuss with students that it is generally considered wrong to profit off of a culture that is not your own.

Ask the class to consider the following question:

- What would make "Tilted Ground" an authentic Indigenous text?

Discuss with students that authentic texts present authentic Indigenous voices, depict themes and issues important to Indigenous peoples, and include respectful portrayals or representations of Indigenous peoples and their traditions and beliefs. In this case, the answer is yes because the author, Sonny Assu, states that he is the great-great grandchild of Chief Billy Assu and is writing about an important time in his Nation's history.

Restate the importance of assessing the authenticity of texts to honour Indigenous voices and the right for Indigenous peoples to reclaim their own stories and histories.

Next, as a class, read the timeline that appears before "Tilted Ground" on pages 28–29 of *This Place: 150 Years Retold*. Have students choose a historical event from the timeline, and briefly research the event and its significance to Canadian history. Have students use the Activity Sheet: Historical Connections (2.2) from lesson 2 to organize their findings.

Alternatively, have students pair up to research the event and its significance to Canadian history. Have groups present their findings to the class.

Before students individually read "Tilted Ground," show them a map of the location of T'sakwa'lutan (also known as Cape Mudge), which is on Quadra Island in what is now British Columbia. The Quadra Island website has a map of the island, including Cape Mudge (go to <http://www.quadraisland.ca/map/quadra-island-map.html#.XcMZgTNKjct>).

TEACHER GUIDE FOR THIS PLACE: 150 YEARS RETOLD © 2021 PORTAGE & MAIN PRESS   ISBN-978-1-77492-017-6

After students have completed the reading, ask comprehension questions to ensure understanding:

- Why do you think it was important that Billy learn to "properly honour the ancestors and visitors" during ceremonies?
- What is the difference between the way the settlers and the Ligwilda'xw Nation treat wealth?
- What did the Superintendent of Indian Affairs of British Columbia say about the potlatch?
- How was the potlatch misinterpreted?
- How did the community resist the potlach ban?
- What did you think of the ending of the story?

APPLY: MINI RESEARCH ASSIGNMENT

Have students choose a leader that is alive today, such as the following:
- current or past chief of a local First Nation
- municipal, provincial, or federal politician
- business, non-profit, or community leader (e.g., a CEO of a well-known company)
- activist (e.g., David Suzuki)
- religious leader
- athlete
- monarch
- scientist
- celebrity or influencer

Students will briefly research this person and then write a compare and contrast essay comparing Chief Billy Assu to the leader of their choice.

Hand out a copy of the Activity Sheet: Compare and Contrast Essay Outline (3.1) and a copy of the Rubric: Compare and Contrast Essay (3.2) to each student.

Alternatively, have students co-construct the rubric with you. Ask them what makes a great compare and contrast essay and write their ideas down on the board. Next, ask them to give a weight to each category to create a graded rubric.

Begin by having students complete their essay outlines as they conduct their research. Then, have students take the point-form notes in their essay outlines and create paragraphs until they have a full essay.

TEACHER GUIDE FOR THIS PLACE: 150 YEARS RETOLD © 2021 PORTAGE & MAIN PRESS ISBN: 978-1-77492-017-6

ASSESS: PEER ASSESSMENT AND COMPARE AND CONTRAST ESSAY RUBRIC

Before students submit their final essays, have them engage in a peer-editing session. As a fair way to distribute the papers, collect all essays and hand them back out in a random order. The essay students receive is the one they will peer edit. Have students read over the essay several times and circle the level of proficiency they would give the student. Make sure students write an explanation for each grade on the back of the rubric. Encourage students to read over the essay a second or third time and fix spelling or grammar errors they notice.

Once students have finished grading their partner's essay, have them return the essay to the author along with the rubric and comments. Allow students time to make changes before submitting their papers for final grading.

TEACHER GUIDE FOR THIS PLACE: 150 YEARS RETOLD © 2021 PORTAGE & MAIN PRESS ISBN-978-1-77492-017-6

Date: _____   Name: _____

COMPARE AND CONTRAST ESSAY OUTLINE

Complete the essay outline as you research. Feel free to use another sheet of paper if you run out of room on this one.

ESSAY COMPONENTS	MY IDEAS
Introduction and background information Introduce the two leaders you are going to compare and contrast. Include background information about each. State your thesis statement.	
Paragraph 1: First similarity and/or difference Include an explanation about how they are similar or different. Give examples from your research. Transition to the next paragraph.	

TEACHER GUIDE FOR THIS PLACE: 150 YEARS RETOLD © 2021 PORTAGE & MAIN PRESS ISBN: 978-1-77492-017-6

Paragraph 2: Second similarity and/or difference Include an explanation about how they are similar or different. Give examples from your research. Transition to the next paragraph.	
Paragraph 3: Third similarity and/or difference Include an explanation about how they are similar or different. Give examples from your research. Transition to the next paragraph.	
Conclusion Restate three key points and thesis while providing closure for the reader and final thoughts.	

TEACHER GUIDE FOR THIS PLACE: 150 YEARS RETOLD © 2021 PORTAGE & MAIN PRESS ISBN: 978-1-77492-017-6

3.1

Date: _____   Name: _____

COMPARE AND CONTRAST ESSAY

TEACHER GUIDE FOR THIS PLACE: 150 YEARS RETOLD © 2021 PORTAGE & MAIN PRESS ISBN: 978-1-77492-017-6

CATEGORY	Excellent	Good	Developing/Needs Improvement
Ideas and Supporting Details /15	The paper compares and contrasts the leaders clearly. The paper points to specific examples to illustrate the comparison. The paper includes only the information relevant to the comparison.	The paper compares and contrasts the leaders clearly, but the supporting information doesn't use specific examples. The paper includes only the information relevant to the comparison.	The paper compares and contrasts the leaders clearly, but the supporting information is incomplete. The paper may include information that is not relevant to the comparison.
Organization & Structure /5	The paper is organized in a logical way that the reader can easily follow. It follows a consistent order when discussing the comparison.	The paper is somewhat organized in a logical way but does not follow a consistent order when discussing the comparison.	The paper is not well organized, and some information is in the wrong section. Some details are not in a logical or expected order, and this distracts the reader.

3.2

CATEGORY	Excellent	Good	Developing/Needs Improvement
Transitions /5	The paper moves smoothly from one idea to the next. The paper uses comparison and contrast transition words to show relationships between ideas. The paper uses a variety of sentence structures and transitions.	The paper moves from one idea to the next, but there is little variety. The paper uses comparison and contrast transition words to show relationships between ideas.	Some transitions work well; but connections between other ideas are fuzzy.
Grammar & Spelling (Conventions) /5	Writer makes no errors in grammar or spelling that distract the reader from the content.	Writer makes a few errors in grammar or spelling that distract the reader from the content.	Writer makes several errors in grammar or spelling that distract the reader from the content.

Total out of 30 marks:

Comments:

TEACHER GUIDE FOR THIS PLACE: 150 YEARS RETOLD © 2021 PORTAGE & MAIN PRESS ISBN: 978-1-77492-017-6

TEACHER GUIDE FOR THIS PLACE: 150 YEARS RETOLD © 2021 PORTAGE & MAIN PRESS   ISBN: 978-1-77492-017-6

WHAT DOES IT MEAN TO HAVE DIFFERENT WORLDVIEWS? (RED CLOUDS)

*CONTENT WARNING: This story contains suicide, murder, violence, and cannibalism.

DURATION
One to three hours

OVERVIEW
Throughout this lesson, students will engage in debate about differing worldviews and values. Students will have the opportunity to be on all sides of the debate, including being a judge.

BACKGROUND
What is a windigo? Jen Storm, the author of "Red Clouds," writes:

> Windigos are spirits that can manifest in different ways. Some manifest on their own to terrorize people. They are tall, ravenous creatures with antlers and long finger-like claws. Some possess humans and turn them into cannibals. During the fur trade era of high starvation and desperation, there were stories of people who turned into a windigo, and that their hunger for human flesh could never be quenched. Red clouds were one sign of windigos coming; their throats made sounds of crushing ice, and they screamed louder than a human possibly could.

> Windigo spirits feast on humans' desperation, fear, selfishness, and at the time of the fur trade, this manifested into physical cannibalism. Today, many say that addiction is the new way a windigo possesses you. It changes you, leaves you unsatiated and needing more. Windigos are never full. They have adapted as we adapted; we have to be aware of that.

> This is, of course, my interpretation and understanding. Other nations have their own windigo stories that I do not know and do not speak for.

It is important to note that in some Indigenous cultures, the windigo is a very real evil that should never be spoken about.

MATERIALS

- copies of *This Place: 150 Years Retold* (one for each student)
- Activity Sheet: Historical Connections (2.2) from lesson 2 (one copy for each student)
- computers/tablets with internet access (optional)
- Information Sheet: Debate Topics and Rotating Roles of Groups (4.1) (one copy for each student)
- Information Sheet: Debate Structure (4.2) (one copy for each student)
- Activity Sheet: Debate Scoresheet (4.3) (one copy for each student)
- Rubric: Written Reflection (4.4) (one copy for each student)
- writing utensils

ACTIVATE: AGREE/DISAGREE STATEMENTS CLASS ACTIVITY

Set up "Agree" and "Disagree" signs at opposite ends of your classroom. Inform students that you are going to read a statement, and if they agree with the statement, they are to go to the "agree" side, and if they disagree they are to go to the "disagree" side. They must choose a side (neutral is not an option). The goal of this activity is to initiate thought about these philosophical topics and their implications.

Read the following statements and wait for students to choose a side before continuing:

1. All humans are naturally good.
2. It is easy to distinguish between right and wrong.
3. The rights of a whole community are more important than the rights of one person.
4. Killing another human being is always wrong (even if done by the state).
5. All humans are equal, and no one should get special privileges.
6. The good of society trumps individual rights.
7. The law should apply the same to everyone.
8. Diversity in thought is a good thing.
9. There are many ways to see a situation.
10. Worldviews different than my own are equally valid.

After reading

- How did you feel when you didn't agree with the majority?
- How did it feel to see that your classmates have different beliefs than you?
- Did anything surprise you?

Solicit student responses. Alternatively, assign the above questions as a written reflection.

TEACHER GUIDE FOR THIS PLACE: 150 YEARS RETOLD © 2021 PORTAGE & MAIN PRESS ISBN-978-1-77492-017-6

ACQUIRE: READ "RED CLOUDS"

As a class, read the author's statement on pages 54–55 of *This Place: 150 Years Retold*, and the author's biography in the "About the Contributors" section, which begins on page 284 in the book.

Ask the class:

- Does anyone know what *cultural appropriation* is?
- What are some examples of cultural appropriation? (e.g., non-Indigenous designers copying traditional Indigenous designs for clothing and selling it for a profit)

Solicit responses. Next, explain that Canadian copyright law protects Indigenous knowledge, including traditional cultural expressions. This means that it is illegal to profit off of the culture of Indigenous peoples in Canada. However, there are some grey areas—for example, some oral stories may be difficult to protect. Discuss with students that it is generally considered wrong to profit off of a culture that is not your own.

Ask the class to consider the following question:

- What would make "Red Clouds" an authentic Indigenous text?

Discuss with students that authentic texts present authentic Indigenous voices, depict themes and issues important to Indigenous peoples, and include respectful portrayals or representations of Indigenous peoples and their traditions and beliefs. In this case, the answer is yes because the author, Jen Storm, identifies as Ojibway and used her own knowledge of oral histories, as well as a historical record of community interviews and historical documents as part of her research.

Restate the importance of assessing the authenticity of texts to honour Indigenous voices and the right for Indigenous peoples to reclaim their own stories and histories.

Next, as a class, read the timeline that appears before "Red Clouds" on pages 54–55 of *This Place: 150 Years Retold*. Have students choose a historical event from the timeline, and briefly research the event and its significance to Canadian history. Students can use the Activity Sheet: Historical Connections (2.2) from lesson 2 to record their findings.

Alternatively, teachers can set up a jigsaw activity where groups of students are given an event from the timeline, and they have the rest of the class to research the significance and present their findings to the rest of the class. This way groups of students will teach the class what they learned and the whole class will gain knowledge about each historical event.

TEACHER GUIDE FOR THIS PLACE: 150 YEARS RETOLD © 2021 PORTAGE & MAIN PRESS ISBN: 978-1-77492-017-6

Before reading "Red Clouds," show students a map of Northwestern Ontario located on Treaty 9 Territory, where the story takes place (go to <https://upload.wikimedia.org/wikipedia/commons/thumb/5/5d/Numbered-Treaties-Map.svg/1024px-Numbered-Treaties-Map.svg.png>).

Have students read "Red Clouds" individually. Once they've finished reading, review the story by having a discussion about worldviews. *Worldview* is the lens through which people see and understand the world. Different societies, past and present, have different ways of viewing the world. Ask students if they can identify the varying worldviews presented in the story.

APPLY: DEBATE

Inform the class that they will be participating in three debates. Students will not get to choose their side of the debate. Instead, they will have the opportunity to be on all sides of a debate—yes, no, and a judge.

Each debate is structured to give groups 15 minutes preparation time to build three arguments. Each argument should have one main point as well as supporting examples. Groups should aim for each argument to be presented in one to two minutes. Divide the class into three groups, and provide each student with a copy of the Information Sheet: Debate Topics and Rotating Roles of Groups (4.1) and Information Sheet: Debate Structure (4.2).

While teams are prepping their arguments, have students who are judges create the scoresheet for the debate that specifies the number of points for each criterion. How judges weigh each item is up to them.

Judges need to come to a consensus about the scoresheet as each judge will use the same rubric. Judges can complete the Activity Sheet: Debate Scoresheet (4.3). For an example, see the thumbnail below.

Sample Scoresheet

Argument #	Team #	Score		Comments
Argument 1	Team Yes	Strength of Argument Presentation Skills Rebuttal Total	/5 /2 /5 /12	

TEACHER GUIDE FOR THIS PLACE: 150 YEARS RETOLD © 2021 PORTAGE & MAIN PRESS ISBN: 978-1-77492-017-6

Before teams present any arguments, ensure the judges inform the teams of the point structure. If needed, allow teams five minutes to revise and practice their arguments based on the score structure.

Teams will present one argument at a time, in alternating order. Time for 30-second rebuttals may be added at the discretion of the teacher. Judges should be reminded to score the teams as the debate is happening.

Once all three rounds of debate are finished, give the judges five minutes to add up the scores, deliberate, and announce a winner.

Conduct the debates as outlined in the Information Sheet: Debate Topics and Rotating Roles of Groups (4.1) and the Information Sheet: Debate Structure (4.2).

ASSESS: WRITTEN REFLECTION

Once the debates have concluded, have students write a one-page written reflection using the following prompt, which can be written on the whiteboard.

Respond thoughtfully and critically to the following prompts:

> *Part 1 (should be one paragraph):*
> *Please reflect on your own role in this debate:*
>
> · *How do you feel about your preparation? Oral presentation? Rebuttals? Overall performance?*
> · *If you were to do this again, how would you do it differently and why?*
>
> *Part 2 (should be another paragraph):*
> *Reflect on what these debates helped you understand about differing worldviews.*
>
> · *How was your own opinion shaped by the arguments in the debates?*
> · *What points were most and least persuasive?*
> · *Do you think that debating these issues helped you understand them better? Why or why not?*
> · *What did you learn, both about the content and the skill of debating, from watching your peers debate?*

Assess students' written reflections using the Rubric: Written Reflection (4.4).

TEACHER GUIDE FOR THIS PLACE: 150 YEARS RETOLD © 2021 PORTAGE & MAIN PRESS ISBN: 978-1-77492-017-6

Date: _____   Name: _____

DEBATE TOPICS AND ROTATING ROLES OF GROUPS

Group A Members:

_____

Group B Members:

_____

Group C Members:

_____

DEBATE 1: Jack Fiddler was just in his killings.	
Group A	Team Yes
Group B	Team No
Group C	Judges
DEBATE 2: The death penalty is right in some circumstances.	
Group A	Team No
Group B	Judges
Group C	Team Yes
DEBATE 3: Sometimes there are appropriate situations in which to break the law.	
Group A	Judges
Group B	Team Yes
Group C	Team No

TEACHER GUIDE FOR THIS PLACE: 150 YEARS RETOLD © 2021 PORTAGE & MAIN PRESS ISBN: 978-1-77492-017-6

4.1

DEBATE STRUCTURE

Prep time: 15 minutes total

Time	Role	Job
15 minutes	Team Yes	Prepare three arguments, including examples and supports for each.
	Team No	Prepare three arguments, including examples and supports for each.
	Judges	Prepare scoresheet and how teams will be marked. Before the debate begins, explain the scoresheet to the teams. Write the scoresheet on the board. Allow teams up to five minutes extra time to adjust arguments to the rubric.

Round One: 8 minutes total

Time	Role	Job
2–3 minutes	Team Yes	Team Yes presents their first argument.
30 seconds	Team No	Team No has 30 seconds to think of a rebuttal to Team Yes's first argument.
30 seconds	Team No	Team No states their rebuttal.
2–3 minutes	Team No	Team No presents their first argument.
30 seconds	Team Yes	Team Yes has 30 seconds to think of a rebuttal to Team No's first argument.
30 seconds	Team Yes	Team Yes states their rebuttal.

TEACHER GUIDE FOR THIS PLACE: 150 YEARS RETOLD © 2021 PORTAGE & MAIN PRESS ISBN: 978-1-77492-017-6

Round Two: 8 minutes total

Time	Role	Job
2–3 minutes	Team No	Team No presents their second argument.
30 seconds	Team Yes	Team Yes has 30 seconds to think of a rebuttal to Team No's second argument.
30 seconds	Team Yes	Team Yes states their rebuttal.
2–3 minutes	Team Yes	Team Yes presents their second argument.
30 seconds	Team No	Team No has 30 seconds to think of a rebuttal to Team Yes's second argument.
30 seconds	Team No	Team No states their rebuttal.

Round Three: 8 minutes total

Time	Role	Job
2–3 minutes	Team Yes	Team Yes presents their final argument.
30 seconds	Team No	Team No has 30 seconds to think of a rebuttal to Team Yes's final argument.
30 seconds	Team No	Team No states their rebuttal.
2–3 minutes	Team No	Team No presents their final argument.
30 seconds	Team Yes	Team Yes has 30 seconds to think of a rebuttal to Team No's final argument.
30 seconds	Team Yes	Team Yes states their rebuttal.

Arguments are now over

Time	Role	Job
5 minutes	Judges	Judges privately add up the points to determine who wins.
1 minute	Judges	Judges present their decision to the class and announce the winner.

TEACHER GUIDE FOR THIS PLACE: 150 YEARS RETOLD © 2021 PORTAGE & MAIN PRESS ISBN: 978-1-77492-017-6

4.2

Date: _____   Name: _____

DEBATE SCORESHEET

TEACHER GUIDE FOR THIS PLACE: 150 YEARS RETOLD © 2021 PORTAGE & MAIN PRESS   ISBN: 978-1-77492-017-6

Argument #	Team	Score		Comments
EXAMPLE Argument 1	Team Yes	Strength of Argument /5 Presentation Skills /5 Rebuttal /5 Total /15		
Argument 1	Team Yes			
	Team No			
Argument 2	Team Yes			
	Team No			
Argument 3	Team Yes			
	Team Yes			

4.3

Date: _____   Name: _____

WRITTEN REFLECTION RUBRIC

	Excellent	Good	Developing/Needs Improvement
Depth of reflection /5	Writing demonstrates an in-depth reflection on topic. Supporting details and/or examples are clearly identified.	Writing demonstrates a general reflection on the topic, including some supporting details and examples.	Writing demonstrates a minimal reflection on the topic including a few supporting details and examples.
Required components /10	Writing surpasses the required components of the assignment.	Writing includes the required components of the assignment.	Writing includes a few of the required components of the assignment.
Structure & Organization /3	Writing is clear, concise, and well organized with the use of excellent sentence/paragraph structure. Thoughts are expressed in a logical manner.	Writing is mostly clear, concise, and organized with the use of excellent sentence/paragraph structure. Thoughts are expressed in a logical manner.	Writing is unclear, and thoughts are not well organized. Thoughts are not expressed in a logical manner.
Grammar /2	There are no spelling or grammar errors.	There are a few spelling or grammatical errors.	There are several spelling or grammatical errors.

Total out of 20 marks:

Comments:

TEACHER GUIDE FOR THIS PLACE: 150 YEARS RETOLD © 2021 PORTAGE & MAIN PRESS ISBN: 978-1-77492-017-6

4.4

TEACHER GUIDE FOR THIS PLACE: 150 YEARS RETOLD © 2021 PORTAGE & MAIN PRESS ISBN: 978-1-77492-017-6

LESSON 5

WHAT ARE EXAMPLES OF INDIGENOUS CONTRIBUTIONS? (PEGGY)

DURATION

Three hours (including research and presentation)

OVERVIEW

Students will learn about the most decorated Indigenous soldier in Canadian history. They will learn about his contributions to Canada during World War I as well as the harsh realities he faced after coming home. Students will then have the opportunity to research another Indigenous contribution and present their findings to the class.

MATERIALS

- copies of *This Place: 150 Years Retold* (one for each student)
- access to the article "Legendary Ojibwa Sniper Unsung Hero of WWI" <https://www.cbc.ca/news/aboriginal/legendary-ojibwa-sniper-unsung-hero-of-ww-i-1.2725241>
- Activity Sheet: Historical Figure, Stages of Life (2.1) from lesson 2 (one copy for each student) (optional)
- Activity Sheet: Historical Connections (2.2) from lesson 2 (one copy for each student) (optional)
- computers/tablets with internet access and slide show software
- projector for presentations
- Rubric: Indigenous Contribution Presentation (5.1) (two copies for each student)
- writing utensils

BACKGROUND

Francis Pegahmagabow somehow managed to slip through the Government of Canada's provision banning minorities from enlisting in World War I to become the most decorated Indigenous soldier in Canadian history. He was one of only 39 in the Canadian Expeditionary Force to be awarded the Military Medal and two bars for valour for his outstanding service as a skilled marksman. However, when Francis returned to Canada after the war, he went back to being discriminated against and faced poverty and legal barriers when trying to provide for his family. Francis died in 1952. In 2006, over 80 years after he served, the military finally decided to recognize him, erecting a monument at CFB Borden with full military honours.

ACTIVATE: MIND MAP

Individually, have students create a mind map to brainstorm as many Indigenous contributions or inventions as they can. A *mind map* is a diagram used to visually organize information. How students organize this information is up to them. After three minutes, have students compare their mind maps with a partner.

ACQUIRE: READ "PEGGY"

As a class, read the author's statement on pages 82–83 of *This Place: 150 Years Retold*, and the author's biography in the "About the Contributors" section, which begins on page 284 in the book.

Ask the class:

- Does anyone know what *cultural appropriation* is?
- What are some examples of cultural appropriation? (e.g., non-Indigenous designers copying traditional Indigenous designs for clothing and selling it for a profit)

Solicit responses. Next, explain that Canadian copyright law protects Indigenous knowledge, including traditional cultural expressions. This means that it is illegal to profit off of the culture of Indigenous peoples in Canada. However, there are some grey areas—for example, some oral stories may be difficult to protect. Discuss with students that it is generally considered wrong to profit off of a culture that is not your own.

Ask the class to consider the following question:

- What would make "Peggy" an authentic Indigenous text?

Discuss with students that authentic texts present authentic Indigenous voices, depict themes and issues important to Indigenous peoples, and include respectful portrayals or representations of Indigenous peoples and their traditions and beliefs. In this case, the answer is yes because the author, David A. Robertson, is a member of Norway House Cree Nation and is writing about an important Indigenous figure in Canadian history.

TEACHER GUIDE FOR THIS PLACE: 150 YEARS RETOLD © 2021 PORTAGE & MAIN PRESS ISBN-978-1-77492-017-6

Restate the importance of assessing the authenticity of texts to honour Indigenous voices and the right for Indigenous peoples to reclaim their own stories and histories.

Next, as a class, read the timeline that appears before "Peggy" on pages 82–83 of *This Place: 150 Years Retold*. If students are not familiar with Francis Pegahmagabow, have them read the CBC article "Legendary Ojibwa Sniper Unsung Hero of WWI" <https://www.cbc.ca/news/aboriginal/legendary-ojibwa-sniper-unsung-hero-of-ww-i-1.2725241> and complete the Activity Sheet: Historical Figure, Stages of Life (2.1) from lesson 2.

Alternatively, have students choose a historical event from the timeline, and briefly research the event and its significance to Canadian history. Students can use the Activity Sheet: Historical Connections (2.2) from lesson 2 to record their findings.

Before students read "Peggy," show them a map of Francis Pegahmagabow's home community, Wasauksing First Nation located in what is now Ontario (go to <https://en.wikipedia.org/wiki/Wasauksing_First_Nation#/media/File:Canada_Southern_Ontario_location_map_2.png>).

Have students individually read "Peggy." After they have finished reading, ask questions to ensure comprehension, such as:

- Why do you think Peggy was such a great sniper?
- How was Peggy treated after the war?
- What was the "new war" that Peggy had to fight back home?

Note: *Meegwetch* on page 89 of "Peggy" means *thank you* in Anishinaabemowin.

APPLY: RESEARCH AN INDIGENOUS CONTRIBUTION AND CREATE A PRESENTATION

Inform students that they will research and create a multimedia presentation (e.g., slide show) about an Indigenous contribution or invention in one of the following areas: medicine, sport, fashion, health and wellness, justice, law, or military. Just as they may have been surprised to learn about Peggy's contributions, there are many other Indigenous contributions that are not common knowledge. This can lead to a discussion about history and whose story gets told. Ask students:

- Why do you think a lot of Canadians are unaware of Indigenous contributions?

Solicit class responses. A possible answer could include Eurocentric curriculum in schools and museums.

Distribute one copy of the Rubric: Indigenous Contribution Presentation (5.1) to each student to explain the assignment. Inform students that possible slides for their presentation could include:

- Title Slide
- Background/History
- Indigenous Contribution
- About the Person
- Significance

Inform the class that their presentations should be between 3–5 minutes in length. They are encouraged to have both words and pictures on each slide.

ASSESS: PEER ASSESSMENT AND CLASS PRESENTATION RUBRIC

Before students present to the class, have them practise with a partner. Each student should provide feedback for their partner in the form of "two stars and a wish." Two stars are two things they enjoyed about the presentation (or strengths of the presentation), and a wish is something that needs improvement.

Once students have finished practising their presentations, allow them time to make revisions based on their peer's feedback before presenting to the whole class. The class should be advised to be good listeners while others are presenting.

As each student presents, make notes and complete the Rubric: Indigenous Contribution Presentation (5.1).

Date: _____   Name: _____

INDIGENOUS CONTRIBUTION PRESENTATION

CATEGORY	Excellent	Good	Developing/Needs Improvement
Knowledge & Understanding /20	The presenter displays an in-depth knowledge about the contribution, its historical context, and its significance.	The presenter displays a decent amount of knowledge about the contribution but may be missing information about historical context or significance.	The presenter displays a limited knowledge about the contribution, its historical context, and its significance.
Visual Appeal /5	The presentation is highly appealing to the audience. Pictures and other multimedia are utilized throughout.	The presentation is somewhat appealing to the audience.	The presentation is not appealing to the audience.
Grammar & Spelling (Conventions) /5	Student makes no errors in grammar or spelling that distract the reader from the content of the multimedia presentation.	Student makes a few errors in grammar or spelling that distract the reader from the content of the multimedia presentation.	Student makes several errors in grammar or spelling that distract the reader from the content on the multimedia presentation.
Presentation Skills /5	The presenter maintains eye contact and appropriate tone/voice throughout the presentation.	The presenter maintains some eye contact and appropriate tone/voice throughout the presentation.	The presenter does not make eye contact and/or does not have appropriate tone/voice throughout the presentation.

Total out of 35 marks: _____

Comments:

TEACHER GUIDE FOR THIS PLACE: 150 YEARS RETOLD © 2021 PORTAGE & MAIN PRESS ISBN: 978-1-77492-017-6

5.1

WHY ARE NAMES IMPORTANT? (ROSIE)

TEACHER GUIDE FOR THIS PLACE: 150 YEARS RETOLD © 2021 PORTAGE & MAIN PRESS   ISBN: 978-1-77492-017-6

DURATION

One hour

OVERVIEW

Students will learn about the significance of names, including their own. Students will read a story about Inuit spirituality and shamanism and then create their own graphic novel scene to tell the story of their name.

MATERIALS

- copies of *This Place: 150 Years Retold* (one for each student)
- Activity Sheet: Historical Connections (2.2) from lesson 2 (one copy for each student)
- Rubric: Graphic Novel Scene (6.1) (two copies for each student) (optional)
- pencil crayons
- art paper
- writing utensils
- loose leaf paper

BACKGROUND

The term *Inuit* is used to describe the Indigenous people who have occupied the most northern parts of Canada, and are distinct from First Nations. The majority of the Inuit population lives in 51 communities spread across Inuit Nunangat, the Inuit homeland encompassing 35 percent of Canada's land mass and 50 percent of its coastline. Due to their relative isolation, roughly 60 percent of Inuit speak Inuktut (the Inuit language).[28]

117

---

28 "About Canadian Inuit." *Inuit Tapiriit Kanatami*. Accessed March 28, 2020. https://www.itk.ca/about-canadian-inuit/

ACTIVATE: THINK/PAIR/SHARE

Note: Students will be asked to share the story of their name in the following activity. There are many reasons why a student may not know the story of their name (e.g., a student may have been adopted or be in foster care), so teachers may want to assign students homework the night before the activity to briefly research their names (where their name originated and the meaning).

Encourage students to share the story of their name (if they know it) with a partner. Topics of discussion might include:

- Who chose their name?
- Are they are named after someone or something?
- Why were they given a particular name?
- What does their name mean?
- Do they have a nickname?

Solicit responses from students.

ACQUIRE: READ "ROSIE"

As a class, read the author's statement on pages 110–111 of *This Place: 150 Years Retold*, and the author's biography in the "About the Contributors" section, which begins on page 284 in the book.

Ask the class:

- Does anyone know what *cultural appropriation* is?
- What are some examples of cultural appropriation? (e.g., non-Indigenous designers copying traditional Indigenous designs for clothing and selling it for a profit)

Solicit responses. Next, explain that Canadian copyright law protects Indigenous knowledge, including traditional cultural expressions. This means that it is illegal to profit off of the culture of Indigenous peoples in Canada. However, there are some grey areas—for example, some oral stories may be difficult to protect. Discuss with students that it is generally considered wrong to profit off of a culture that is not your own.

Ask the class to consider the following question:

- What would make "Rosie" an authentic Indigenous text?

Discuss with students that authentic texts present authentic Indigenous voices, depict themes and issues important to Indigenous peoples, and include respectful portrayals or representations of Indigenous peoples and their traditions and beliefs. In this case, the answer is yes because the author, Rachel Qitsualik-Tinsley, identifies as being of Inuit-Cree ancestry and

TEACHER GUIDE FOR THIS PLACE: 150 YEARS RETOLD © 2021 PORTAGE & MAIN PRESS ISBN 978-1-77492-017-6 co-author Sean Quitsualik-Tinsley identifies as being of Scottish-Mowhawk ancestry, and they are writing about Inuit spirituality.

Restate the importance of assessing the authenticity of texts to honour Indigenous voices and the right for Indigenous peoples to reclaim their own stories and histories.

Next, as a class, read the timeline that appears before "Rosie" on pages 110–111. Have students choose a historical event from the timeline, and briefly research the event and its significance to Canadian history. Students can use the Activity Sheet: Historical Connections (2.2) from lesson 2 to record their findings.

Before students read "Rosie," show them a map of the traditional territory of Inuit, which is located in the Northernmost regions of what is now Canada. Inuit territories include Nunavut, Nunavik (also referred to as Northern Quebec), Nunatsiavut, NunatuKavut (also referred to as Labrador), and parts of the Northwestern Territories (go to <https://www.aadnc-aandc.gc.ca/Map/irs/mp/map_en/accessibility/en/Inuit_Nunangat_EN.html>).

Have students individually read "Rosie." After they have finished reading, ask questions to ensure comprehension, such as:

- Who is narrating the story?
- What gifts did Rosie have?
- What is the significance of names in this story?

APPLY: GRAPHIC NOVEL SCENE

Have students create their own graphic novel scene, relating to the story of how they got their name, or the origin of their name. Alternately, students can create a graphic novel scene related to an event in their family history.

Before they begin, ask students what they think should be included in the rubric that will be used to grade their assignment. Co-construct a rubric with the class. Alternatively, use the Rubric: Graphic Novel Scene (6.1).

Students can begin planning their graphic novel scenes on sheet of loose leaf, including all the parts of a graphic novel they learned about in lesson 1. Students should write a brief description of the scene they would like to draw for each panel. Once they have each of their scenes planned students should write the dialogue, thoughts, and other elements that they want to include. See lesson 1 for more information on creating a graphic novel scene.

TEACHER GUIDE FOR THIS PLACE: 150 YEARS RETOLD © 2021 PORTAGE & MAIN PRESS ISBN-978-1-77492-017-6

ASSESS: GRAPHIC NOVEL SCENE RUBRIC

Before students submit their graphic novel scenes, have them engage in a peer-editing session. Distribute one copy of the Rubric: Graphic Novel Scene (6.1) to each student, and have students exchange their graphic novel scene with a partner. Have students review their partner's scene several times, and circle the level of proficiency they would give the student. Make sure students write an explanation for the grade they gave each category, using the back of the rubric to jot down their comments and suggestions for improvement. Remind students that constructive criticism is not personal and should include both positive comments and comments that suggest in a friendly manner an area needing improvement.

Have students revise their work and create a final version on art paper before submitting the graphic novel scenes to you for final grading. Use the Rubric: Graphic Novel Scene (6.1) to assess students' work.

Date: _____   Name: _____

GRAPHIC NOVEL SCENE

CATEGORY	Excellent	Good	Developing/Needs Improvement
Comic Story Structure /10	The story is very well-organized. One idea or scene follows another in a logical sequence with clear transitions.	The story is pretty well-organized. One idea or scene may seem out of place. Clear transitions are used.	The story is hard to follow. The transitions are sometimes not clear.
Visual Appeal /10	Carefully chosen images help the reader understand the action and emotions in the story.	Most of the images help the reader understand the story. One or two are unrelated or confusing.	Comic includes many images that do not relate to the story and confuse readers.
Grammar & Spelling (Conventions) /5	Writer makes no errors in grammar or spelling that distract the reader from the content of the graphic novel scene.	Writer makes a few errors in grammar or spelling that distract the reader from the content of the graphic novel scene.	Writer makes several errors in grammar or spelling that distract the reader from the content of the graphic novel scene.
Effort /5	Final product is completed. Pride in one's work, proper time management, and adequate planning is evident.	Final product is short, and more effort could have been placed on time management and/or adequate planning.	Final product is incomplete. Pride in one's work, proper time management, or adequate planning is not evident.

Mark out of 30:

Comments:

TEACHER GUIDE FOR THIS PLACE: 150 YEARS RETOLD © 2021 PORTAGE & MAIN PRESS ISBN-978-1-77492-017-6

6.1

TEACHER GUIDE FOR THIS PLACE: 150 YEARS RETOLD © 2021 PORTAGE & MAIN PRESS ISBN-978-1-77492-017-6

LESSON 7

HOW CAN WE PRACTISE WELLNESS? (NIMKII)

*CONTENT WARNING: This story contains physical abuse, stolen children, sexual abuse, and suicide.

DURATION
Two hours

OVERVIEW
Schools often don't explicitly teach students how to be *well*. Throughout this lesson, students will read a story about a Sixties Scoop survivor's experiences and then learn about Indigenous theories of wellness relating to all parts of the self: physical, mental, emotional, and spiritual. Students will set goals in each category in order to facilitate holism, balance, and wellness in their lives. The goal is that students learn the value of self-care, and why it is especially important while learning about difficult topics.

MATERIALS
- copies of *This Place: 150 Years Retold* (one copy for each student)
- whiteboard or chart paper
- markers
- Activity Sheet: Historical Connections (2.2) from lesson 2 (one copy for each student)
- computer/tablet with internet access
- Activity Sheet: Medicine Wheel Goal Setting (7.1) (one copy for each student)
- scrap paper
- writing utensils

BACKGROUND

There are more Indigenous children in Canada's child welfare system today than there were at the height of the residential school era. Canada's child welfare policy, along with the Sixties Scoop when thousands of Indigenous children were sent into non-Indigenous foster care homes, has had devastating effects on Indigenous communities. These children experienced loss of culture, language, and identity. Many also endured physical, emotional, and sexual abuse. Today, the legacies of residential schools and the Sixties Scoop are still felt, and many survivors are turning to traditional healing methods to cope.

ACTIVATE: SELF-CARE WHOLE-CLASS DISCUSSION

Explain to students that this lesson's reading touches upon difficult topics such as physical abuse, children forcibly taken from their families, sexual abuse, and suicide. While it is important not to shy away from these often-triggering topics, it is equally important that we make sure we have the tools to take care of ourselves and make sure we are well. Provide a list of mental health resources that students can access both in school and in the community. Review the list of resources with students and discuss healthy coping skills before and after reading the story. Healthy coping skills can be simply defined as healthy ways to deal with stress (e.g., deep breathing, taking a break, talking about our feelings).

Begin the discussion by asking:

- What does it mean to be *well*?

Write students' answers on the whiteboard, so students have a visual for how wellness might look and feel. Inform students that wellness looks and feels different to different people, and that it is important for us to know what wellness looks and feels like for us personally.

ACQUIRE: READ "NIMKII"

As a class, read the author's statement on pages 138–139 of *This Place: 150 Years Retold*, and the author's biography in the "About the Contributors" section, which begins on page 284 in the book.

Ask the class:

- Does anyone know what *cultural appropriation* is?
- What are some examples of cultural appropriation? (e.g., non-Indigenous designers copying traditional Indigenous designs for clothing and selling it for a profit)

TEACHER GUIDE FOR THIS PLACE: 150 YEARS RETOLD © 2021 PORTAGE & MAIN PRESS   ISBN: 978-1-77492-017-6

Solicit responses. Next, explain that Canadian copyright law protects Indigenous knowledge, including traditional cultural expressions. This means that it is illegal to profit off of the culture of Indigenous peoples in Canada. However, there are some grey areas—for example, some oral stories may be difficult to protect. Discuss with students that it is generally considered wrong to profit off of a culture that is not your own.

Ask the class to consider the following question:

· What would make "Nimkii" an authentic Indigenous text?

Discuss with students that authentic texts present authentic Indigenous voices, depict themes and issues important to Indigenous peoples, and include respectful portrayals or representations of Indigenous peoples and their traditions and beliefs. In this case, the answer is yes because the author, Kateri Akiwenzie-Damm, is from Chippewas of Newash First Nation and is writing a story to honour the Indigenous children who were taken away by the government.

Restate the importance of assessing the authenticity of texts to honour Indigenous voices and the right for Indigenous peoples to reclaim their own stories and histories.

Next, as a class, read the timeline that appears before "Nimkii" on pages 138–139 of *This Place: 150 Years Retold*. Have students choose a historical event from the timeline and briefly research the event and its significance to Canadian history. Students can use the Activity Sheet: Historical Connections (2.2) from lesson 2 to organize their findings.

Before students read "Nimkii," show them a map of the Wabaseemoong reserve located in Ontario. This is where parts of the story take place (go to <https://goo.gl/maps/Us3d8aKRAc39dsqX8>).

Have students read "Nimkii." After they have finished reading, ask questions to ensure comprehension, such as the following:

· What are some ways Nimkii coped with the trauma of being away from her family?
· How did the community fight against the state taking their children in the end?

ACQUIRE: MEDICINE WHEEL WELLNESS LESSON
Invite an Elder to speak to the class about the medicine wheel and its significance in Indigenous culture. See "Inviting an Elder Into Your Learning Space" on page 8 for suggestions for inviting Elders to speak to students.

TEACHER GUIDE FOR THIS PLACE: 150 YEARS RETOLD © 2021 PORTAGE & MAIN PRESS ISBN: 978-1-77492-017-6

If this option is not available, there are many online resources that can help you explain the medicine wheel to your students, such as "The Seven Lessons of the Medicine Wheel" by Kelly J. Beaulieu.[29]

Hand out a copy of the Activity Sheet: Medicine Wheel Goal Setting (7.1) to each student. On the whiteboard or chart paper, draw a large medicine wheel and label the four quadrants: "Physical," "Mental," "Spiritual," and "Emotional."

Explain that the four quadrants can represent many things, such as the four directions, the four phases of life, or the four sacred medicines.

Explain to students that they will use the medicine wheel to examine and think about the four parts of the self, according to Indigenous ways of knowing—physical, mental, spiritual, and emotional—and how it is important for the parts to be balanced if we truly want to be well. Advise students that we are also doing this activity to ensure that we can look after ourselves while learning about difficult topics, such as those presented in "Nimkii."

Provide students with information regarding the mental health supports that are available to them in the school and community. Consider inviting a school counsellor to teach students about mental health and healthy coping skills. As a class, brainstorm a list of healthy coping skills and record the list on the white board. Students can use this list to choose the skills they are most likely to use to set goals.

Have students set goals for themselves that fit each quadrant and write the goals on scrap paper. Explain that some goals may fit in two or more quadrants but to just pick the category that makes the most sense for them. It may be helpful to give some examples of goals for each quadrant:

- physical goals (health, fitness): I will lift weights once per week.
- spiritual goals (religious, focusing on self, family, community, or anything that makes our "spirit" happy): I will practise my culture with my family once a month.
- mental goals (knowledge, school): I want to learn about outer space.
- emotional (mental health): I will practise deep breathing when I feel stressed.

Students should set at least three goals for each of the four quadrants.

TEACHER GUIDE FOR THIS PLACE: 150 YEARS RETOLD © 2021 PORTAGE & MAIN PRESS ISBN: 978-1-77492-017-6

---

29   Beaulieu, Kelly J. "The Seven Lessons of the Medicine Wheel." *Say Magazine.* https://saymag.com/the-seven-lessons-of-the-medicine-wheel/

APPLY: MEDICINE WHEEL GOAL SETTING ACTIVITY

Once students have at least three goals in each category, have them transform their goals into "SMART" goals. SMART stands for Specific, Measurable, Attainable, Realistic, and Time-bound. Write the following example on the white board.

- Physical goal: I will eat healthy food.

Discuss with students how this goal is not SMART (e.g., specific, measurable, time-bound). Have students give suggestions on how to make this goal SMART. For example:

- I will eat three servings of vegetables every day.
OR
- I will limit myself to one sugary snack a day.

Have students fill in the Activity Sheet: Medicine Wheel Goal Setting (7.1) with their goals for the year using the SMART goal format.

Finally, have students colour the four quadrants (physical = black, spiritual = yellow, mental = white, emotional = red).

ASSESS: MEDICINE WHEEL ASSESSMENT

Since this assignment is highly personal, it is often difficult to grade. An option is to have students read out three of their goals to you, so you can assess if the goals are "SMART" goals:

- Specific
- Measurable
- Achievable
- Realistic
- Time-bound

An example of a SMART goal is as follows:

- I will weight train once per week.

It is specific (instead of saying something vague like "I want to be stronger."); it is measurable, meaning you can easily identify if you accomplished the goal or not; it is achievable and realistic (you're not saying you are going to win a weight-lifting competition anytime soon, unless you are close to doing that already!); and it is time-bound, meaning you will do this every day, week, month, or year.

TEACHER GUIDE FOR THIS PLACE: 150 YEARS RETOLD © 2021 PORTAGE & MAIN PRESS ISBN: 978-1-77492-017-6

EXTENSION: CHECK-IN ACTIVITY

Throughout the year, you can also use the medicine wheel as a tool to check in on students' wellness.

Model how to do the check-in with your students. On the whiteboard, draw a large medicine wheel. Label the quadrants with the four parts of the self: "Physical," "Mental," "Spiritual," and "Emotional."

Explain to students that you are going to rate your own feelings of wellness today using the four categories. Draw a dot where you feel your own level of wellness is at today. Dots near the centre of the circle indicate you are not doing too well in that category, whereas dots near the outer edge of the circle indicate you feel well in that category. Connect your dots to form a circle shape. Circles that look like the medicine wheel indicate you are feeling well and balanced in all areas, whereas circles that look out of balance indicate you need to work on some areas today. See the following illustration as an example.

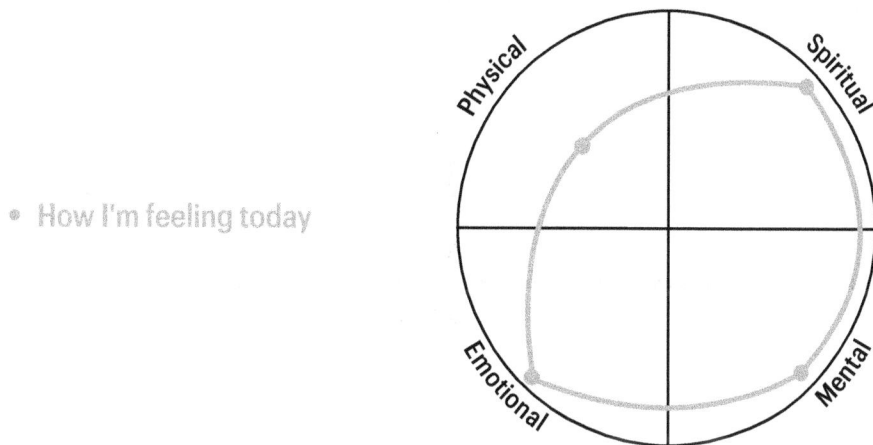

How I'm feeling today

Meet one-on-one with each student to discuss their wellness levels, and have a conversation about how they can increase their wellness in areas that they rate lower. For example, if a student is giving their physical wellness a low rating, have a discussion about why that is and what they can do to improve their wellness for tomorrow. For example, if a student often feels tired, they may want to work on going to bed earlier.

TEACHER GUIDE FOR THIS PLACE: 150 YEARS RETOLD © 2021 PORTAGE & MAIN PRESS ISBN: 978-1-77492-017-6

Date: _____   Name: _____

MEDICINE WHEEL GOAL SETTING

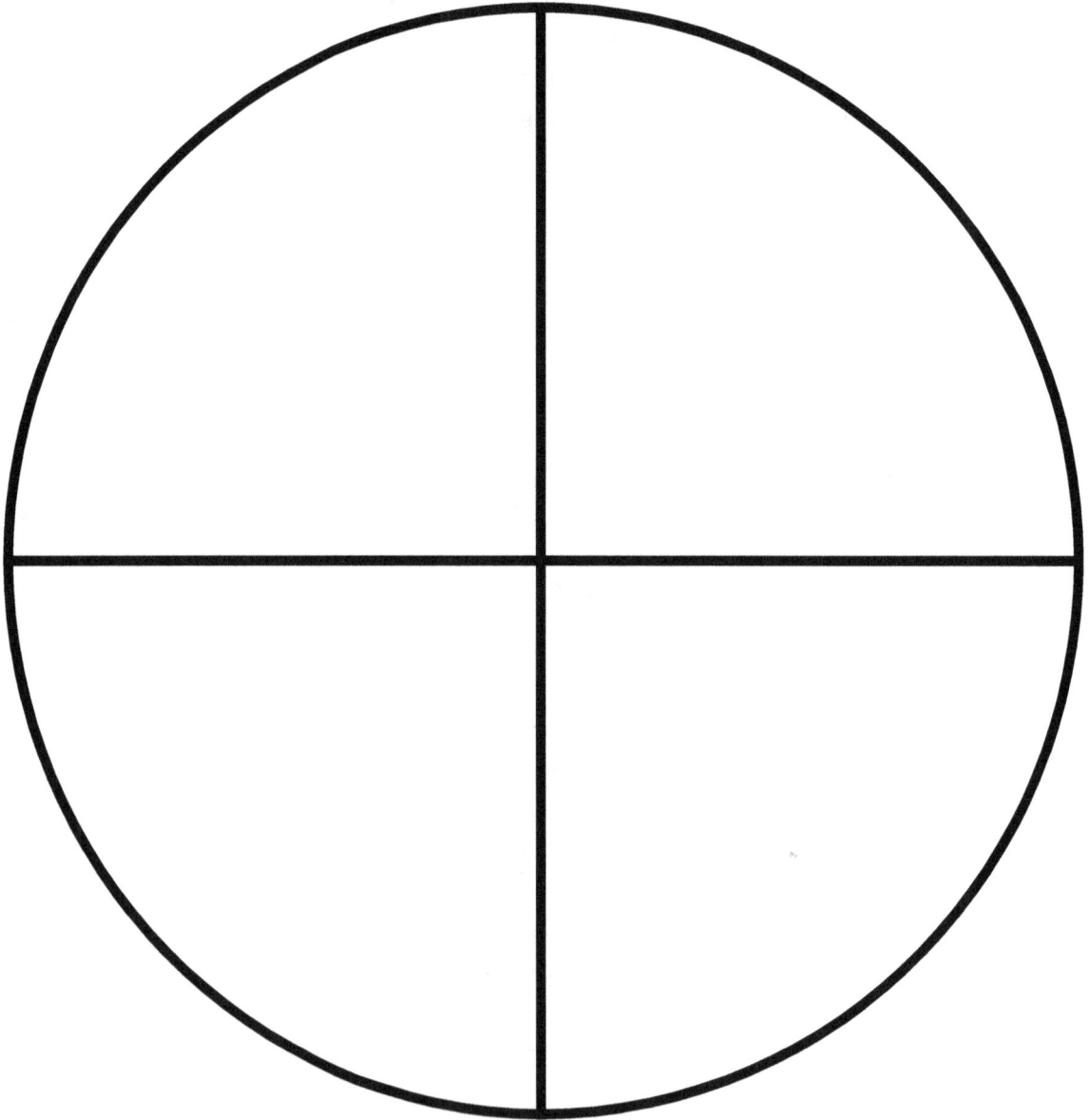

TEACHER GUIDE FOR THIS PLACE: 150 YEARS RETOLD © 2021 PORTAGE & MAIN PRESS   ISBN: 978-1-77492-017-6

7.1

WHAT MAKES AN EFFECTIVE SPEECH? (LIKE A RAZOR SLASH)

DURATION

One to two hours

OVERVIEW

Students will engage in a gallery walk activity where they will summarize and reflect on some important speeches in history.

MATERIALS

- copies of *This Place: 150 Years Retold* (one for each student)
- whiteboard or chart paper
- markers
- Activity Sheet: Historical Figure, Stages of Life (2.1) from lesson 2 (one copy for each student) OR Activity Sheet: Historical Connections (2.2) from lesson 2 (one copy for each student)
- computers/tablets with internet access for viewing video speeches
- several printed copies of Sojourner Truth's speech: "Ar'n't I A Woman? Ain't I a Woman?" <https://sojournertruthmemorial.org/sojourner-truth/her-words> or other speeches
- Activity Sheet: Gallery Walk Worksheet (8.1)

TEACHER GUIDE FOR THIS PLACE: 150 YEARS RETOLD © 2021 PORTAGE & MAIN PRESS ISBN: 978-1-77492-017-6

BACKGROUND

The significance of the Mackenzie Valley pipeline project cannot be understated. The gas pipeline was going to be the biggest pipeline project in Canada as it would have taken gas from the Beaufort Sea to markets in Canada and the United States. Canadian judge, Mr. Justice Thomas Berger was appointed to examine the impacts that the pipeline would have on the local people. Berger travelled and met with Dene, Inuit, and Métis leaders—including Chief Frank T'Seleie, who presented a powerful speech about the devasting impacts the pipeline would have on the local people, land, and animals. Chief Frank T'Seleie's speech was successful in delaying and then ultimately stopping the pipeline from being built.

ACTIVATE: SPEECH BRAINSTORM

Ask students if they've heard any moving speeches lately. Then ask them what they think makes a speech great. Write their answers on the whiteboard or chart paper. Possible answers include: effective opening (hook), relating to the audience, honesty, humour, etc.

ACQUIRE: READ "LIKE A RAZOR SLASH" AND OTHER SPEECHES (GALLERY-WALK FORMAT)

As a class, read the author's statement on pages 167–169 of *This Place: 150 Years Retold*, and the author's biography in the "About the Contributors" section, which begins on page 284 in the book.

Ask the class:

- Does anyone know what *cultural appropriation* is?
- What are some examples of cultural appropriation? (e.g., non-Indigenous designers copying traditional Indigenous designs for clothing and selling it for a profit)

Solicit responses. Next, explain that Canadian copyright law protects Indigenous knowledge, including traditional cultural expressions. This means that it is illegal to profit off of the culture of Indigenous peoples in Canada. However, there are some grey areas—for example, some oral stories may be difficult to protect. Discuss with students that it is generally considered wrong to profit off of a culture that is not your own.

Ask the class to consider the following question:

- What would make "Like a Razor Slash" an authentic Indigenous text?

Discuss with students that authentic texts present authentic Indigenous voices, depict themes and issues important to Indigenous peoples, and include respectful portrayals or representations of Indigenous peoples and their traditions and beliefs. In this case, the answer is yes because the author, Richard Van Camp, is from Tlicho Nation in the Northwest Territories and is writing a story about an important Indigenous historical figure in the territory.

TEACHER GUIDE FOR THIS PLACE: 150 YEARS RETOLD © 2021 PORTAGE & MAIN PRESS ISBN: 978-1-77492-017-6

Restate the importance of assessing the authenticity of texts to honour Indigenous voices and the right for Indigenous peoples to reclaim their own stories and histories.

Next, as a class, read the timeline that appears before "Like a Razor Slash" on pages 167–169 of *This Place: 150 Years Retold*. If students are not familiar with Chief Frank T'Seleie, have students briefly research the historical figure and complete the Activity Sheet: Historical Figure, Stages of Life (2.1) from lesson 2.

Alternatively, have students choose a historical event from the timeline, and briefly research the event and its significance to Canadian history. Students can use the Activity Sheet: Historical Connections (2.2) from lesson 2 to record their findings.

APPLY: GALLERY WALK

Organize the classroom tables/desks into four stations. Place materials at each station as follows:

Station 1:
- several copies of *This Place: 150 Years Retold*, so students can read "Like a Razor Slash"
- a computer/tablet with internet access set up to view a map of Fort Good Hope, NWT showing where the story took place <https://goo.gl/maps/rQhM58eyhGPErtICA>

Station 2:
- a computer/tablet with internet access set up to watch Martin Luther King Jr.'s famous "I Had a Dream Speech" <https://www.youtube.com/watch?v=I47Y6VHc3Ms>

Station 3:
- a computer/tablet with internet access set up to watch "Autumn Pelletier 13-year-old water advocate addresses the UN" <https://www.youtube.com/watch?v=zg6osr38oic>

Station 4:
- several printed copies of Sojourner Truth's speech: "Ar'n't I A Woman? Ain't I a Woman?" <https://sojournertruthmemorial.org/sojourner-truth/her-words/>

Divide the class into the four groups, and explain that they will be reading and watching some important speeches. Hand out a copy of the Activity Sheet: Gallery Walk Worksheet (8.1) to each student. Explain to students that they are to spend 15 minutes at each station to watch or read the speech and complete the Activity Sheet: Gallery Walk Worksheet (8.1). Their job is to summarize the material and then write a short response.

Write some prompts on the whiteboard so students understand what they should be writing about. The following prompts can be used to guide students' writing:

TEACHER GUIDE FOR THIS PLACE: 150 YEARS RETOLD © 2021 PORTAGE & MAIN PRESS ISBN: 978-1-77492-017-6

Summary
- Who wrote this speech?
- What was the speech about? What was the message?
- Quote a phrase that stood out to you.
- What was the mood of the speech?
- Did the orator use any figurative language?

My Response
- What did you think of the speech?
- Did any part resonate with you?
- Do you think this was an effective speech? What made it effective?
- Do you relate to anything mentioned in the speech?

If students finish before their time at their station is up, they can discuss the material with their group members.

ASSESS: GALLERY-WALK GRADING SYSTEM

Have students hand in their gallery walk activity sheets at the end of the class. Use the grading system below to assess their summaries and responses. Both Summary and My Reponses are out of three marks, for a total out of six marks. Grade each as follows:

- Three marks: Thorough description, analysis, and reflection
- Two marks: Developing, needs more specific examples and personal reflection
- One mark: Brief, lacks detail

TEACHER GUIDE FOR THIS PLACE: 150 YEARS RETOLD © 2021 PORTAGE & MAIN PRESS ISBN: 978-1-77492-017-6

Date: _____   Name: _____

GALLERY-WALK WORKSHEET

Station	Summary	My Response
Speech 1:		
Speech 2:		

TEACHER GUIDE FOR THIS PLACE: 150 YEARS RETOLD © 2021 PORTAGE & MAIN PRESS   ISBN: 978-1-77492-017-6

Speech 3:		
Speech 4:		

TEACHER GUIDE FOR THIS PLACE: 150 YEARS RETOLD © 2021 PORTAGE & MAIN PRESS ISBN: 978-1-77492-017-6

8.1

WHY IS RESOURCE DEVELOPMENT IN INDIGENOUS COMMUNITIES CONTROVERSIAL? (MIGWITE'TMEG: WE REMEMBER IT)

TEACHER GUIDE FOR THIS PLACE: 150 YEARS RETOLD © 2021 PORTAGE & MAIN PRESS ISBN: 978-1-77492-017-6

DURATION

Two+ hours

OVERVIEW

This lesson focuses on the topic of resource development in First Nations communities. Students will read a story about the fishing raids that took place in Listuguj, Quebec in the 1980s and relate this to current topics in Indigenous industry. Students will research a resource development project in an Indigenous community and present their findings regarding the history and controversies in essay format.

MATERIALS

- copies of *This Place: 150 Years Retold* (one for each student)
- computers/tablets with internet access
- projector
- Activity Sheet: Historical Connections (2.2) (one copy for each student)
- Rubric: Research Essay (9.1) (two copies for each student)

BACKGROUND

In June of 1981, the Quebec Provincial Police and fisheries officers raided Restigouche Reserve, arrested residents, and seized their boats in order to prevent them from commercially fishing salmon. At issue were the salmon-fishing and self-determination rights of the Mi'gmaq. Because salmon has traditionally been a source of food and income for the Mi'gmaq, the province's decision to restrict fishing angered the Mi'maq fishers and led to tension between the Mi'gmaq and police. Eventually the convictions were overturned and in 1999 the Supreme Court recognized the Mi'gmaq's right to fish.

ACTIVATE: VIEW THE CBC DOCUMENTARY *COLONIZATION ROAD*

Explain to the class that they will be learning about resource development in Indigenous communities and the effects that so-called "progress" has on the lives of Indigenous peoples.

Show the following video to the class:

- <https://www.cbc.ca/firsthand/episodes/colonization-road>
"Colonization Road." *CBC Firsthand*. (44:07).

This documentary takes viewers on a journey to the beginning of the creation of Canada to show how treaties are the foundation of Canadian law and how they have been repeatedly broken. Colonization roads are roads that settlers have built on Indigenous territories across Canada to connect them to resource development at the expense of First Nation communities. Narrated by Indigenous comedian Ryan McMahon, this documentary explores how colonization "has led not only to the growth of Canada, but the very real cost of that growth and how honouring the treaties, foundational to this place we all call home, can lead to a decolonized Canada as long as the waters flow."[30]

ACQUIRE: READ "MIGWITE'TMEG: WE REMEMBER IT"

As a class, read the author's statement on pages 193–195 of *This Place: 150 Years Retold*, and the author's biography in the "About the Contributors" section, which begins on page 284 in the book.

Ask the class:

- Does anyone know what *cultural appropriation* is?
- What are some examples of cultural appropriation? (e.g., non-Indigenous design)

Solicit responses. Next, explain that Canadian copyright law protects Indigenous knowledge, including traditional cultural expressions. This means that it is illegal to profit off of the culture of Indigenous peoples in Canada. However, there are some grey areas—for example, some oral stories may be difficult to protect. Discuss with students that it is generally considered wrong to profit off of a culture that is not your own.

---

30 *Colonization Road*, directed by Michelle St. John, written by Ryan McMahon, Jordan O'Connor, and Michelle St. John, featuring Ryan McMahon, aired June 17, 2019, on CBC-TV, https://www.cbc.ca/firsthand/episodes/colonization-road.

TEACHER GUIDE FOR THIS PLACE: 150 YEARS RETOLD © 2021 PORTAGE & MAIN PRESS ISBN: 978-1-77492-017-6

Ask the class to consider the following question:

· What would make "Migwite'tmeg: We Remember It" an authentic Indigenous text?

Discuss with students that authentic texts present authentic Indigenous voices, depict themes and issues important to Indigenous peoples, and include respectful portrayals or representations of Indigenous peoples and their traditions and beliefs. In this case, the answer is yes because the author, Brandon Mitchell, is from Listuguj, Quebec and is writing a story about the government raids that happened there.

Restate the importance of assessing the authenticity of texts to honour Indigenous voices and the right for Indigenous peoples to reclaim their own stories and histories.

Next, as a class, read the timeline that appears before "Migwite'tmeg: We Remember It" on pages 193–195 of *This Place: 150 Years Retold*. Have students choose a historical event from the timeline, and briefly research the event and its significance to Canadian history. Students can use the Activity Sheet: Historical Connections (2.2) from lesson 2 to record their findings.

Have students individually read "Migwite'tmeg: We Remember It". Once students have finished reading, discuss as a class the similarities between the story in the graphic novel and the documentary.

Also, show students a map locating Listuguj, Quebec, the community where the story takes place (for example, go to <https://www.cbc.ca/news/canada/montreal/listuguj-mi-kmaq-64m-land-settlement-approved-by-ottawa-1.3066365>).

APPLY: WRITE AN ESSAY ABOUT RESOURCES IN FIRST NATIONS COMMUNITIES
Tell students they will research a specific Indigenous community and how it has been directly impacted by resource development. Encourage students with connections to First Nations communities to choose the community that they are connected to.

Alternatively, assign students a resource sector (e.g., mining, oil, hydro, forestry, fisheries, green energy) and have them research the impact development has had on First Nations communities. Students will need to take notes based on their research. Provide students with an essay graphic organizer they are familiar with.

Go over the Rubric: Research Essay (9.1) with students before they begin writing their essays, so they know what is expected of them.

TEACHER GUIDE FOR THIS PLACE: 150 YEARS RETOLD © 2021 PORTAGE & MAIN PRESS ISBN: 978-1-77492-017-6

ASSESS: PEER ASSESSMENT AND ESSAY RUBRIC

Before students submit their final essays, have them engage in a peer-editing session. As a fair way to distribute the essays, collect all essays and hand them back out in a random order. The essay students receive is the one they will peer edit. Hand out copies of the Rubric: Research Essay (9.1) and have students read over the essay several times and circle the level of proficiency they would give the student. Make sure students write an explanation about why they gave each category the grade they did (have students use the back of the rubric to jot down their comments). Encourage students to fix spelling or grammar errors as they read.

Once students have finished grading their partner's essay, have them hand back the essay to the author along with the rubric and comments. Allow students time to revise their essays before submitting the paper for final grading.

Date: _____   Name: _____

RESEARCH ESSAY

Categories	Excellent	Good	Developing/Needs Improvement
Knowledge & Understanding (**Knowledge of Key Concepts**) **/20**	The student demonstrates thorough and sophisticated knowledge of concepts and fully explores and analyzes the topic in depth.	The student demonstrates strong knowledge of concepts and explores the topic in depth.	The student demonstrates some knowledge of concepts and attempts to explore the topic in depth.
Quality of Research **/20**	The paper is exceptionally researched, contains two peer reviewed sources, presented in a logical manner.	The information relates to the main topic. Paper, is well-researched in detail and from reliable sources.	The information relates to the main topic, but few details and/or examples are given. Shows a limited variety of sources.
Convention (**Use of Conventions, Vocabulary, and Grammar**) **/10**	The student uses conventions with a high degree of effectiveness.	The student uses conventions with considerable effectiveness.	The student uses conventions with some effectiveness.
MLA format **/10**	MLA format is followed throughout the whole paper. Sources are cited correctly.	MLA format is mostly followed throughout the paper. Sources are cited correctly.	Some characteristics of MLA format are adhered to. Sources may not be cited correctly.

Total marks out of 60:

Comments:

TEACHER GUIDE FOR THIS PLACE: 150 YEARS RETOLD © 2021 PORTAGE & MAIN PRESS ISBN-978-1-77492-017-6

TEACHER GUIDE FOR THIS PLACE: 150 YEARS RETOLD © 2021 PORTAGE & MAIN PRESS ISBN: 978-1-77492-017-6

LESSON 10

WHAT IS NON-VIOLENT RESISTANCE? (WARRIOR NATION)

DURATION
Two to three hours

OVERVIEW
Students will learn about the Oka Crisis and its significance to Indigenous resistance movements throughout Canada and the United States. Students will research an Indigenous resistance movement and present their findings to the class.

MATERIALS
- copies of *This Place: 150 Years Retold* (one for each student)
- Activity Sheet: Historical Connections (2.2) from lesson 2 (one copy for each student)
- computers/tablets with slide show software and internet access
- projector for presentations
- Rubric: Non-Violent Resistance Presentation (10.1) (two copies for each student)
- writing utensils

BACKGROUND
The Oka Crisis, also known as the Mohawk Resistance, was a 78-day standoff in 1990 between Mohawk protesters, police, and the Canadian military. The standoff was over a land dispute that included the proposed expansion of a golf course and development of condominiums on land that included a sacred Mohawk burial ground. Eventually, the golf course expansion was cancelled.

ACTIVATE: WHOLE-CLASS DISCUSSION

As a class, discuss non-violent resistance. Begin by asking:

- What do you think *non-violent resistance* means?
- Can you think of any examples of non-violent resistance?

Explain that non-violent resistance is the process of achieving goals (often political or social) by means of non-violent encounters including but not limited to protests, civil disobedience, and art activism.

ACQUIRE: READ "WARRIOR NATION"

As a class, read the author's statement on pages 220–221 of *This Place: 150 Years Retold*, and the author's biography in the "About the Contributors" section, which begins on page 284 in the book.

Ask the class:

- Does anyone know what *cultural appropriation* is?
- What are some examples of cultural appropriation? (e.g., non-Indigenous designers copying traditional Indigenous designs for clothing and selling it for a profit)

Solicit responses. Next, explain that Canadian copyright law protects Indigenous knowledge, including traditional cultural expressions. This means that it is illegal to profit off of the culture of Indigenous peoples in Canada. However, there are some grey areas—for example, some oral stories may be difficult to protect. Discuss with students that it is generally considered wrong to profit off of a culture that is not your own.

Ask the class to consider the following question:

- What would make "Warrior Nation" an authentic Indigenous text?

Discuss with students that authentic texts present authentic Indigenous voices, depict themes and issues important to Indigenous peoples, and include respectful portrayals or representations of Indigenous peoples and their traditions and beliefs. In this case, the answer is yes because the author, Niigaanwewidam James Sinclair, identifies as Anishinaabe and is writing a story about the Oka resistance.

Restate the importance of assessing the authenticity of texts to honour Indigenous voices and the right for Indigenous peoples to reclaim their own stories and histories.

Next, as a class, read the author's statement and timeline that appear before "Warrior Nation" on pages 220–221 of *This Place: 150 Years Retold*. Have students choose a historical event from the timeline, and briefly research the event and its significance to Canadian history. Students can use the Activity Sheet: Historical Connections (2.2) from lesson 2 to record their findings.

TEACHER GUIDE FOR THIS PLACE: 150 YEARS RETOLD © 2021 PORTAGE & MAIN PRESS ISBN: 978-1-77492-017-6

Before reading "Warrior Nation," ensure that all students are familiar with the *Meech Lake Accord*. If a student researched this for their historical event, have them share what they learned with the class.

Also, show students a map locating the Oka village in Quebec, where the resistance in the story took place (for example, go to <https://www.rcinet.ca/en/2018/07/09/on-this-day-shooting-death-police-indian-canada-history-july-11-1990-the-crisis-and-death-at-oka/>).

Have students individually read "Warrior Nation." After they have finished reading, ask comprehension questions to ensure understanding:

- Why were Indigenous leaders such as Elijah Harper against the *Meech Lake Accord*?
- How did Indigenous peoples demonstrate resistance in the Oka Crisis?
- Why was the land important to the Haudenosaunee (pronounced *ho-dee-no-shownie*)
- What do you think the effects of the Oka resistance were? Do you think we still feel these effects today?

APPLY: RESEARCH AN INDIGENOUS RESISTANCE MOVEMENT

In groups of two to three, have students research an Indigenous resistance movement or protest, such as one of the following:

- Oka Crisis (1990)
- Idle No More (2013-present)
- Standing Rock (2016-2017)
- Red River Resistance (1870)
- Northwest Resistance (1885)
- Ipperwash Crisis and the death of Dudley George (1995)
- Burnt Church, New Brunswick fisheries dispute (2000)
- Caledonia, Ontario occupation (2006)

Have students prepare a multimedia presentation (e.g., slide show) to teach the class about the movement they chose on a first-come first-serve basis. Show them the Rubric: Non-Violent Resistance Presentation (10.1) before they get started so they know what is expected of them.

ASSESS: PEER FEEDBACK, PRESENTATIONS, AND PRESENTATION RUBRIC

Before students present in front of the class, have them practise with a partner. Each student should provide feedback in the form of "two stars and a wish." Two stars are two things they enjoyed about the presentation (or strengths of the presentation), and one wish is something that needs improvement.

TEACHER GUIDE FOR THIS PLACE: 150 YEARS RETOLD © 2021 PORTAGE & MAIN PRESS ISBN: 978-1-77492-017-6

Students should be given time to revise their presentations based on their peer's feedback before presenting to the whole class. Encourage students to be good listeners while others are presenting.

As each student presents, make notes and complete the Rubric: Indigenous Contribution Presentation (10.1).

TEACHER GUIDE FOR THIS PLACE: 150 YEARS RETOLD © 2021 PORTAGE & MAIN PRESS ISBN: 978-1-77492-017-6

Date: _____   Name: _____

NON-VIOLENT RESISTANCE PRESENTATION

CATEGORY	Excellent	Good	Developing/Needs Improvement
Knowledge & Understanding /20	The presenter displays an in-depth knowledge about the resistance and specific acts of non-violence, its historical context, and its significance.	The presenter displays a decent amount of knowledge about the resistance and acts of non-violence, but may be missing information about historical context or significance.	The presenter displays a limited knowledge about the resistance and specific acts of non-violence, its historical context, and its significance.
Visual Appeal /5	The presentation is highly appealing to the audience. Pictures and other multimedia are utilized throughout.	The presentation is somewhat appealing to the audience.	The presentation is not appealing to the audience.
Grammar & Spelling (Conventions) /5	Writer makes no errors in grammar or spelling that distract the reader from the content on the multimedia presentation.	Writer makes a few errors in grammar or spelling that distract the reader from the content on the multimedia presentation.	Writer makes several errors in grammar or spelling that distract the reader from the content on the multimedia presentation.
Presentation Skills /5	The presenter maintains eye contact and appropriate tone/ voice throughout the presentation.	The presenter maintains some eye contact and appropriate tone/ voice throughout the presentation.	The presenter does not make eye contact and/or does not have appropriate tone/ voice throughout the presentation.

Total out of 35 marks:

Comments:

TEACHER GUIDE FOR THIS PLACE: 150 YEARS RETOLD © 2021 PORTAGE & MAIN PRESS ISBN: 978-1-77492-017-6

10.1

WHAT WILL THE FUTURE BE LIKE? (KITASKÎNAW 2350)

DURATION

Two+ hours (depending on short story writing time)

OVERVIEW

This lesson will focus on Indigenous futurisms. Students will read a story about a future shaped by Indigenous peoples set in the year 2350. Students will engage in a carousel activity where they will have the opportunity to envision a utopian future in which Indigenous rights and sovereignty are upheld and celebrated. Students will then write their own futurism short story.

MATERIALS

- copies of *This Place: 150 Years Retold* (one for each student)
- chart paper
- markers
- Activity Sheet: Historical Connections (2.2) from lesson 2 (one copy for each student)
- Activity Sheet: Short Story Plot Diagram (11.1) (one copy for each student)
- Rubric: Short Story (11.2) (one copy for each student)
- writing utensils

BACKGROUND

Indigenous futurism is an exciting new genre that aims to change the narrative of Indigenous peoples as existing only in the past. Indigenous futurisms imagine a world where Indigenous knowledge and sovereignty fuse with technology and modernism to reshape society as we know it.

TEACHER GUIDE FOR THIS PLACE: 150 YEARS RETOLD © 2021 PORTAGE & MAIN PRESS ISBN: 978-1-77492-017-6

ACTIVATE: CAROUSEL ACTIVITY

A carousel activity is a great way for students to brainstorm and built off each other's answers. To begin, arrange the tables/desks into four stations. Provide a sheet of chart paper and several markers at each station. Divide students into four groups and explain that today's lesson focuses on dreaming about the future. Tell them that they will have five minutes at each station to answer the question and jot down their thoughts as they discuss with their group. Once the five minutes is up, students will move to the next station, and discuss/answer the next question.

On the chart paper at each station, write the following corresponding question (station 1 will have question 1, station 2 will have question 2, etc.).

1. What are examples of futurisms that you've read/watched/listened to?
2. What are common characteristics of futurisms?
3. How do you envision the future of society in Canada in 2100?
4. Envision a utopia: How could Canada have been different today, if the spirit and intent of the treaties were honoured and Indigenous peoples were equal partners in the founding of Canada?

ACQUIRE: READ "KITASKÎNAW 2350"

As a class, read the author's statement on pages 247–248 of *This Place: 150 Years Retold*, and the author's biography in the "About the Contributors" section, which begins on page 284 in the book.

Ask the class:

- Does anyone know what *cultural appropriation* is?
- What are some examples of cultural appropriation? (e.g., non-Indigenous designers copying traditional Indigenous designs for clothing and selling it for a profit)

Solicit responses. Next, explain that Canadian copyright law protects Indigenous knowledge, including traditional cultural expressions. This means that it is illegal to profit off of the culture of Indigenous peoples in Canada. However, there are some grey areas—for example, some oral stories may be difficult to protect. Discuss with students that it is generally considered wrong to profit off of a culture that is not your own.

Ask the class to consider the following question:

- What would make "kitaskînaw 2350" an authentic Indigenous text?

Discuss with students that authentic texts present authentic Indigenous voices, depict themes and issues important to Indigenous peoples, and include respectful portrayals or representations of Indigenous peoples and their traditions and beliefs. In this case, the answer is yes because the author, Chelsea Vowel, identifies as Métis and is writing an Indigenous futurism story.

TEACHER GUIDE FOR THIS PLACE: 150 YEARS RETOLD © 2021 PORTAGE & MAIN PRESS ISBN: 978-1-77492-017-6

Restate the importance of assessing the authenticity of texts to honour Indigenous voices and the right for Indigenous peoples to reclaim their own stories and histories.

Next, as a class, read the timeline that appears before "kitaskînaw 2350" on pages 247–248 of *This Place: 150 Years Retold*. Have students choose a historical event from the timeline, and briefly research the event and its significance to Canadian history. Students can use the Activity Sheet: Historical Connections (2.2) from lesson 2 to organize their findings.

Have students individually read "kitaskînaw 2350." Ask the class comprehension questions to check for understanding, such as:

- Why do you think the author began the story with "the Returners" coming back to Earth? Why do you think they left in the first place?
- Why does Capan get sent to the past? What is she supposed to learn about?
- How do the author and illustrator depict the future in this story? (i.e., what does it look like?)
- How does the author critique the present? What does she say about the relationship between Indigenous and non-Indigenous people?

APPLY: WRITE YOUR OWN FUTURISM SHORT STORY

Inform students that today they will have the opportunity to write their own futurism short story. A futurism is a story that takes place in the future. They can choose the year they want their story to take place in. Review the parts of a short story as a class, and have students complete the Activity Sheet: Short Story Plot Diagram (11.1) to help them plan their story. Show the students the Rubric: Short Story (11.2) so they know what is expected of them. Once the plot diagram is complete, they can begin to write their stories out on a computer or loose leaf. Give students one to two classes to plan and write their stories.

ASSESS: PEER ASSESSMENT AND SHORT STORY RUBRIC

Before students submit their final short stories, have them engage in a peer-editing session. As a fair way to distribute the stories, collect all short stories and hand them back out in a random order. The story the students receive is the one they will peer edit. Hand out copies of the Rubric: Short Story (11.2) and have students read over the story several times and circle the level of proficiency they would give the student. Make sure students write an explanation about why they gave each category the grade they did (have students use the back of the rubric to jot down their comments). Encourage students to fix spelling or grammar errors as they read.

Once students have finished giving feedback on their partner's story, have them hand back the story to their partner along with the rubric and comments. Allow students time to revise their stories before submitting them for final grading.

TEACHER GUIDE FOR THIS PLACE: 150 YEARS RETOLD © 2021 PORTAGE & MAIN PRESS ISBN: 978-1-77492-017-6

SHORT STORY PLOT DIAGRAM

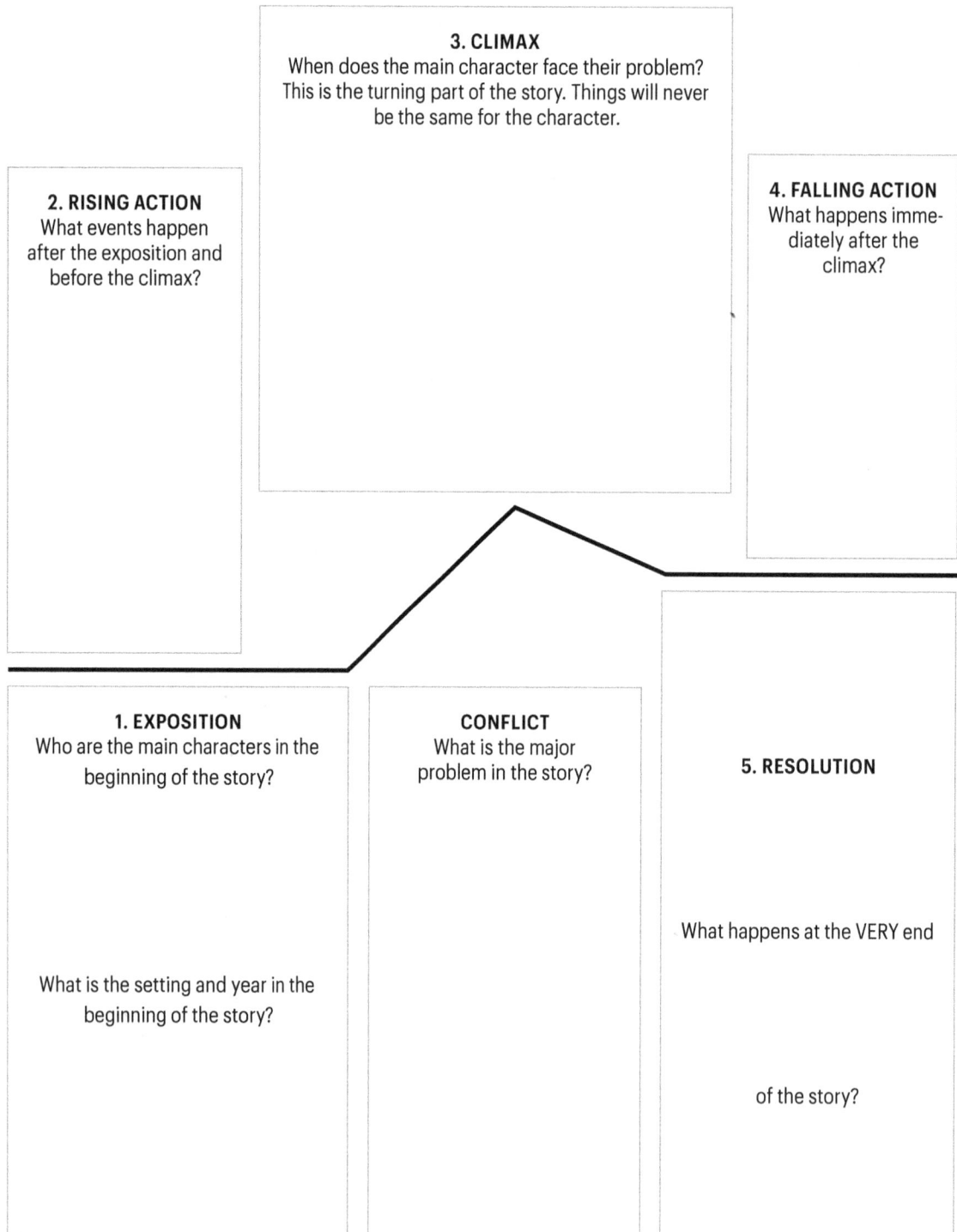

3. CLIMAX
When does the main character face their problem?
This is the turning part of the story. Things will never
be the same for the character.

2. RISING ACTION
What events happen
after the exposition and
before the climax?

4. FALLING ACTION
What happens imme-
diately after the
climax?

1. EXPOSITION
Who are the main characters in the
beginning of the story?

What is the setting and year in the
beginning of the story?

CONFLICT
What is the major
problem in the story?

5. RESOLUTION

What happens at the VERY end

of the story?

TEACHER GUIDE FOR THIS PLACE: 150 YEARS RETOLD © 2021 PORTAGE & MAIN PRESS   ISBN: 978-1-77492-017-6

11.1

Date: _____   Name: _____

SHORT STORY

CATEGORY	Excellent	Good	Developing/Needs Improvement
Ideas & Supporting Details /20	The short story has an elaborate beginning, middle and end. Many vivid, descriptive words are used to describe the setting, characters and conflict.	The short story includes a beginning, middle and end. The author describes the setting, characters and conflict effectively.	The short story is missing one of the following: beginning, middle, or end. The author attempts to describe the setting, characters, and conflict but details are missing.
Organization & Structure /5	The story is organized in a logical way that the reader can easily follow.	The story is somewhat organized in a logical way but it is hard to follow the story line.	The story is not well organized. Some details are not in a logical or expected order, and this distracts the reader.
Grammar & Spelling (Conventions) /5	Writer makes no errors in grammar or spelling that distract the reader from the content.	Writer makes a few errors in grammar or spelling that distract the reader from the content.	Writer makes several errors in grammar or spelling that distract the reader from the content.

Total out of 30 marks:

Comments:

TEACHER GUIDE FOR THIS PLACE: 150 YEARS RETOLD © 2021 PORTAGE & MAIN PRESS ISBN: 978-1-77492-017-6

LESSON 12

WHAT MAKES A PODCAST EFFECTIVE?

DURATION
Two to three hours

OVERVIEW
This lesson is adaptable for any of the podcast episodes in the series and can be used as a stand-alone lesson or while reading *This Place: 150 Years Retold*, the graphic novel. Students will reflect on previous knowledge regarding the historical event in the podcast, analyze various elements of the podcast, and write a podcast review.

MATERIALS
- computers/tablets with internet connection and speakers
- Activity Sheet: KWL Chart (12.1) (one copy for each student)
- Information Sheet: Podcast Review Criteria (12.2) (one copy for each student)
- Rubric: Podcast Review (12.3) (one copy for each student)

BACKGROUND
A podcast is an audio show available for listening via online streaming or downloading. This podcast is a ten-part adaptation of the acclaimed graphic novel *This Place: 150 Years Retold*, bringing the stories of Indigenous resistance and resilience to life! Each episode includes a dramatization and interview with the author and is sure to deepen understanding of Indigenous history and the history of the country known as Canada.

ACTIVATE: FILL IN THE ACTIVITY SHEET: KWL CHART

Prior to having students listen to the podcast episode, share with them the story introduction (found on the *CBC Listen* website at <https://www.cbc.ca/books/thisplace/this-place-podcast-hosted-by-rosanna-deerchild-explores-150-years-of-indigenous-resistance-and-resilience-1.6073883>). Distribute one copy of the Activity Sheet: KWL Chart (12.1) to each student. Based on the information in the introduction, have students write down the historical event that the podcast dramatizes at the top of the page where it says "Topic." Next, have students complete the first two columns of the KWL chart by listing what they know about the topic in the first column and what they want to learn about the topic in the second column. Students will have the opportunity to fill out the third column after they listen to the episode.

ACQUIRE: LISTEN

Have students either listen to the podcast episode independently (as homework, or in class on their own devices using headphones) or listen together as a class. All ten episodes of the podcast are available for free listening on *CBC Listen* at <https://www.cbc.ca/books/thisplace/this-place-podcast-hosted-by-rosanna-deerchild-explores-150-years-of-indigenous-resistance-and-resilience-1.6073883>.

APPLY: PODCAST ANALYSIS

Once students have listened to the podcast episode, have them complete the third column in their KWL charts, writing down everything they learned about the topic from the podcast.

Next, inform students that they will be writing a podcast review based on the episode they just listened to. Explain that a podcast review is like a movie or book review where the author describes and analyzes the content, style, and overall merit of the work. Distribute one copy of the Information Sheet: Podcast Review Criteria (12.2) to each student and explain that their podcast reviews should follow its structure. Advise students whether they are expected to complete Paragraph 4: Compare and Contrast. This will depend on whether they have read the corresponding story in *This Place: 150 Years Retold*, the graphic novel.

Ensure that students are familiar with the concepts and terminology used in the Information Sheet: Podcast Review Criteria (12.2). For instance:

- "dramatization" refers to "the act of converting a narrative in some other form (e.g., a novel or a short story) into a drama for stage, screen, or radio."[31] Dramatic elements, including voice, movement, music, and sound effects, are added to create the effect of something happening in real time. If students are unfamiliar with the term, provide the definition and then either give examples or have students give examples of dramatization found in the episode.

---

31 *Oxford Reference*, s.v. "dramatization," accessed August 10, 2021, https://www.oxfordreference.com/view/10.1093/oi/authority.20110803095730232.

TEACHER GUIDE FOR THIS PLACE: 150 YEARS RETOLD © 2021 PORTAGE & MAIN PRESS ISBN: 978-1-77492-017-6

- "counter-narrative" refers to "the narratives that arise from the vantage point of those who have been historically marginalized."[32] The purpose of a counter-narrative is to resist dominant narratives that disempower and limit the agency of communities. If students are unfamiliar with the term, provide the definition and then discuss with students how the story in the podcast can fit the definition of a counter-narrative.

Once students understand the expectations of the assignment, have students listen to the podcast episode again, either independently or together as a class, so they can find answers to the questions on the Information Sheet: Podcast Review Criteria (12.2). Encourage students to add notes to the "Learned" column of their KWL charts (12.1) and use these KWL charts as they write their podcast reviews.

ASSESS: PODCAST REVIEW RUBRIC

Assess the students' podcast reviews using the Rubric: Podcast Review (12.3).

TEACHER GUIDE FOR THIS PLACE: 150 YEARS RETOLD © 2021 PORTAGE & MAIN PRESS ISBN: 978-1-77492-017-6

32 Mora, Raúl A., "Counter-Narrative," *Key Concepts in Intercultural Dialogue*, no. 36 (2014), https://centerforinterculturaldialogue. org/2014/10/13/key-concept-36-counter-narrative-by-raul-a-mora/.

Date: _____   Name: _____

KWL CHART

TOPIC_____

Use this chart to write notes about what you already know about the topic in the "Know" column and what you want to know in the "Want to Know" column. After listening to the podcast, complete the "Learned" column.

KNOW	WANT TO KNOW	LEARNED

TEACHER GUIDE FOR THIS PLACE: 150 YEARS RETOLD © 2021 PORTAGE & MAIN PRESS ISBN: 978-1-77492-017-6

12.1

PODCAST REVIEW CRITERIA

Your podcast review should contain the following information:

PARAGRAPH 1: INTRODUCTION ANALYSIS

- What information was included in the introduction to the episode?
- Was the introduction catchy or clever? How so?
- Did the introduction state the purpose of the podcast? What is it?

PARAGRAPH 2: DRAMATIZATION

- What dramatic elements did the podcast include?
- How did the dramatic re-enactment influence your understanding of the story?

PARAGRAPH 3: PURPOSE

- What counter-narrative is this story offering?
- How does the story demonstrate resistance?
- What inspired the author to write about this story?

PARAGRAPH 4: COMPARE AND CONTRAST

(optional; for students who have read the story in the graphic novel)

- What did you learn through the episode that wasn't included in the written story?
- Did you enjoy listening to the story or reading the story better?

PARAGRAPH 5: OVERALL OPINION

- Do you think the historical figure at the centre of this podcast should be celebrated in Canadian history? Why or why not?
- What questions do you still have about this story?
- Would you recommend this podcast to others? Why or why not?

TEACHER GUIDE FOR THIS PLACE: 150 YEARS RETOLD © 2021 PORTAGE & MAIN PRESS   ISBN: 978-1-77492-017-6

12.2

Date: _____   Name: _____

PODCAST REVIEW

CATEGORY	Excellent	Good	Developing/Needs Improvement
Depth of Reflection /5	Writing demonstrates an in-depth reflection on topic. Supporting details and/or examples are clearly identified.	Writing demonstrates a general reflection on the topic, including some supporting details and examples.	Writing demonstrates a minimal reflection on the topic, including a few supporting details and examples.
Required Components /10	Writing surpasses the required components of the assignment.	Writing includes the required components of the assignment.	Writing includes a few components of the assignment.
Structure & Organization /3	Writing is clear, concise, and well organized with the use of excellent sentence/paragraph structure. Thoughts are expressed in a logical manner.	Writing is mostly clear, concise, and organized with the use of effective sentence/paragraph structure. Thoughts are expressed in a logical manner.	Writing is unclear, and thoughts are not well organized. Thoughts are not expressed in a logical manner.
Grammar /2	There are no spelling or grammatical errors.	There are a few spelling or grammatical errors.	There are several spelling or grammatical errors.

Total out of 20 marks:

Comments: